FRED DIBNAH
Steeplejack

by
F. Dibnah

Line One publishing ltd

To Alison
With Love

ISBN 0 907036 17 1

Published by
Line One Publishing Limited
Bayshill House
Bayshill Road
Cheltenham
Glos.
GL50 3AA

Contents

All photographs are from the author's private collection.
Cover photographs by Peter Nicholson.

A superb example of the art of erecting staging. Depicted at the top of the 200 ft chimney at Maple Mill, Oldham.

Chapter 1

Early Days

When I was a little lad I went to school like all little lads do. In those days the main road from Bolton to Manchester was made of blue cobbled stones and had two tram tracks down middle. I never liked going to school so me mother used to shove me on a tram, which then went rattling along the road. For the next mile and a half there were five chimney stacks to be counted and where I got off stood a great mass of them belching black smoke.

Every so often ladders painted bright red with men going up and down them appeared on the chimneys. When you are seven, years old a man at the top of a 200ft high stack looks like someone from outer space. Those fellows really fascinated me, though the only two facts I knew about them were that they had red ladders and wore flat caps.

Then one morning after prayers, our headmaster announced he had a special treat for us kids. We were going to watch one of them great chimneys fall. In strict single file we were marched to a field at the back of the school and told to sit perfectly still. I remember we sat all morning, full of tension, waiting for that chimney to topple. It were still standing when we went home to midday dinner. On our return the stack lay on the ground and we had missed everything...

"I never saw it come down," I told my parents. "I never did."

My school days rolled on and I kept seeing more red ladders on the chimneys around me. I never knew who owned them until years later. By then me father had an allotment beside a greyhound track on a site which had once been occupied by an old colliery. The chimney was standing and the chap who owned the site, which also had dog kennels and a cafe, decided it were time to get rid of the stack.

He engaged the services of some sort of mountain men from a place called Bacup. These characters arrived with ladders that had once been red but were now very wishy-washy. Anyway the men began by knocking off the top of the chimney. After that they chopped a big hole in the bottom and put in blocks of wood. I did not know what was going on though that were no matter. You see I had a ringside seat being allowed in the allotment with me father.

It were a right gloomy Sunday during winter and when the mountain men lit their fire under chimney the flames danced in the dark. The site owner also put on all the lights round his greyhound tracks which made us very excited. Then things began to go wrong. This was because not many chimneys were knocked down in those days and no one really knew what they were doing. The chimney came down sure enough, but it did not go right. I vividly recall the stack cutting the dog kennels in half and chopping a corner off the cafe. In addition it ripped down every power cable and all the lights went out. There were utter panic.

My next craze was to get a bike because everyone else seemed to have one. Even though me father slaved in a bleach factory and me mother at the gas works we never had any real money. Therefore a bike was something to be made by visiting tips. If you were lucky there would be a frame here and a couple of wheels somewhere else. After that came a pair of handlebars and you did not worry too much about brakes in them days.

The point was my bike enabled me to get about a bit searching for more things. By a fantastic stroke of luck I found an old pair of binoculars. I would then travel to and climb on top of the Earl of Bradford's slag heap. From there on clear summer nights I could survey the edges of Bolton and especially all them chimney stacks. It had to be summer for in winter you could not see for heavy smoke.

One clear summer night I spotted some strange black lines across the top of a chimney. They belonged to somebody's staging and next night I cycled right across town to have a closer look at what were going on. As I got nearer I saw red ladders with the name 'John Faulkner, Manchester' on their sides. Well you know how some fellows follow pop groups or football teams. From that evening my hero was John Faulkner.

I followed John Faulkner and his men who climbed chimneys around Bolton and Manchester. To my mind they did things right compared to others. Their staging when it appeared on top of a stack was square, symmetrical and solid looking with ropes coiled up all nice and neat. The others had crooked and funny looking staging with bits of rope blowing in the wind.

This were when I was still at school though not doing very well. I was no good at reading and writing so they put the likes of me in the art group. There we painted vases of flowers and bowls of apples. Also when our teacher felt like it we would go for walks with our drawing books. Of course you could not go anywhere without seeing chimneys. Not only did I draw all the chimneys but I put in red ladders and staging.

"What have you put those in for?" my teacher would ask and I answered, "It were in my mind."

During my school holidays spent chimney watching I had to go home around about midday and take me father's dinner to the bleach works. He worked in an unbelievable place. Every corner you turned there were a steam engine throbbing away and driving some piece of shafting. They had big steam engines for the main heavy bits and little ones stuck in different places. More steam came out of the roof than went through the pipes and every evening there were adverts in the local paper for stokers.

Me father worked at a contraption called a beetling machine which were a creation of the devil. If you study a piece of cloth just after weaving it is full of protruding fibres that have to be flattened. The modern method is to run the cloth through steam-heated rollers but in them days beetling machines were used. They were monstrous with cast iron frames and rollers, beech beams and oak noggins.

Also, there were no safety guards round anything. As the big cast iron rollers with all the oak noggins turned, the cloth was dragged through the machine. Apart from the dirt flying about, the noise was terrible and you could not hear yourself speak. No one can describe what it sounded like though some literary character called it 'Dante's Inferno'.

To think that me father spent 40 uncomplaining years working one of those creations. Below the floor where he worked there were a river alive with rats. They raced about below him and would climb boldly up to have a go at his dinner when I arrived with it. Two big chimneys above the bleach works belched out black smoke day and night. Nowt was ever done about anything as the owners were also big on the town council.

When me dad realised I had this strange interest in steeple jacking he told me the following tale.

"During war," he said, "some jacks came to repair tops of chimneys. Well they got up all right and fixed their staging. However the chimneys were kept working and hot due to the war effort. There must have been thousands of tons of coal burnt below them."

"Couldn't have been comfortable up top." I said.

"It were not," me father agreed. "One lot of staging went on fire and was all glowing like a beacon in the blackout. Everyone were powerless to do anything about it until the flames fizzled out."

"Fantastic!" I said.

But there were no vacancies for would-be steeple jacks or chimney sweeps when I went to the Youth Employment Bureau as it was called in those days. The chap behind the counter said,

"Well now, we have one very good job available. Undertaking."

Sometimes I wish I had taken that up because, whatever else happens, undertakers are never out of business.

Anyway I was sent to some funeral parlour where the undertaker looked like a corpse himself. With a funny sort of smile he opened a door and beckoned me into a room filled with trestles and coffins. While looking around I thought 'This isn't for me.' So I acted real dumb and was sent back to the Youth Employment Bureau.

"Well now," said the chap behind the counter, "we have another good opportunity available as a jobbing joiner. Trouble is, six other lads after it and they're already walking there."

"I have me bike," I said like Norman Tebbit.

The joiner gaffer was called Mr. Rawlinson who later let me call him Bill—God rest his soul. He was a nice man and by way of a test asked me if I knew what a tenon saw was. I told him me grandfather had left me one of them which went down well.

The long and the short of it was I got the job and for that first four years everything were marvellous. One day Mr. Rawlinson asked me if I had ever done any pointing. We had just put a window frame in but as for working with mortar he had not a clue.

After doing that window, I had to point a whole garden wall which took me about a fortnight. The old bird at whose house I worked was so impressed she asked if I could do the same to her gable ends. They were three stories high and I did not have anything like the tackle to get up there. Mr. Rawlinson took me to one side like I was his friend.

"I don't want to turn down work," he said. "Can you do it?"

"It's elementary steeple jacking." I assured him, "and I've studied all them techniques."

How I managed it with his short ladders and bits of board lashed together I shall never know. I did however and Mr. Rawlinson realised it were like another extension to his joinery business. He now went in for what he called 'Property Repairing' with me pointing one gable end after another.

Yet, as I said, he were a good man and like most others in those days did not have much money. What he did have was an old Wolsley Hornet with a leather body and what they called a sunshine roof. That meant the rain came straight through. Eventually Mr. Rawlinson filled it full of wood shavings from his planing machine, put a sheet of felt over the top and tarred the whole lot. That were high technology for them days.

He also had a trailer with Austin artillery wheels from the 1920's. Mr. Rawlinson never once painted them and the rust had been rampant for

November 1963—Bolton Parish church.

years. Although each wheel were made of two metal plates welded together you could see daylight through both of them. I sort of accepted anything then. There was not even a toilet at his works—you had to pee in a corner of the yard.

How we worked was I loaded up the trailer then he drove me to the job. Afterwards Mr. Rawlinson went elsewhere and I had to find my own way back to the yard. That was where he made his mistake as far as I were concerned. While working at joinery, I would be studying the nearest chimney, particularly if it had red ladders on it. I still hankered after being a steeple jack in a flat cap going up and down them red ladders.

But I were employed by Mr. Rawlinson and I worried about his trailer. He did overload it. Sometimes he filled that trailer with six cubic yards of solid wood all wet through as well. Anyway I loaded up the trailer one winter morning and he set off on his own for Ashton-under-Lyne. Normally he were back about half five yet, when I locked up after six, Mr. Rawlinson had not yet returned.

The Wolsley was there next morning but no trailer. Mr. Rawlinson told me he had been zooming up the road from Bolton to Bury when one of the wheels sort of finally gave up the ghost. The rim with the tyre on had gone past him while the trailer with its load ran on to the grass verge and collapsed.

"I never did get to Ashton-under-Lyne," Mr. Rawlinson told me.

"What now?" I asked.

"Oh, I tried to get two new wheels from one scrapman," he replied, "but a quid was too much. Fortunately I've found another axle with wheels on it. Bit of a complicated job though I'm sure you'll manage."

Which I did. I had been with him the longest though every now and then he would sign on somebody if we were a bit busy—to help me out of the muck like. One day a peculiar fellow came along. He were a strange sort of man who smoked a briar wood pipe and wore a long black overcoat.

"I want you," Mr. Rawlinson told me, "to keep an eye on that fellow. He likes having a drink, y'know."

'Nothing unusual about that,' I thought, but said nothing.

There were a handcart in the yard for local jobs almost as knackered as the trailer. One day the new man and I had to load it with two lengths of guttering, two ladders and our tool bags. We were about half way up a hill when the new fellow takes a hammer out of his bag and proceeds to smash one wheel. Of course the cart falls over with me left looking at it.

The fellow went to the nearest phonebox, rang Mr. Rawlinson and said the old cart had collapsed. This meant the gaffer coming out in his car and trailer. Mr Rawlinson did not seem too surprised about the hand cart and I kept my mouth shut.

I continued to keep my mouth shut about the new fellow who did have a drink problem. Early each afternoon he would say to me,

"Just going for a box of matches."

It always took him an hour or two to get them. Once I was alone on some roof when I heard the ladder shaking and clattering. It were the new fellow and he was properly topped up. In the end I had to send for Mr. Rawlinson to help get him down to the ground. And that were the end of him as well.

Mr. Rawlinson had yet another man come to work for us. One day this new fellow and I were proceeding somewhere when we saw an enormous chimney out in the country. It was 262ft tall, had red ladders stuck up the side and staging round the top. Those staging planks were 22ft long yet they looked like matchsticks.

"I'd love to climb up there." I said.

'You'd never do it." said this fellow.

So I laid him a wager of ten bob that I would not only get to the top but also leave proof of my climb.

The next job we had were at a park site. In the park keeper's hut I found a large union jack about 8ft tall and 14ft long. Without saying anything I rolled up the flag and shoved it inside my jacket. It made a bit of a bulge and on my way home a young slater I knew asked what it were, like.

"It's a union jack," I said. "I'm going to climb that chimney back there and fly the flag from one of the two lightning conductors. For a bet."

"Better still," said the slater, "I've got another union jack at home. I'll give you mine as well." You see, he were as mad as me.

Now the chimney was situated a long way from the works with its flue running underground through a wood. There were also a bit of a stone wall round the base to keep out foolhardy people. So I had to do the job at night and on arriving at the stack I found they had taken away the first 16ft ladder.

I tied an old nut to a piece of string and threw it over the bottom rung of the second ladder. Using the string, I pulled a rope through then proceeded to climb the main stack. On reaching the top I tied the union jacks to the lightning conductors, came down and went home rather sooty like. Of course there were a lot of "Where have you been?" and all that, but I did not let on to me parents.

Next day in the evening paper, there was a magnificent picture of the chimney with the two union jacks fluttering from the top. For some unknown reason the authorities blamed it on the Manchester University students who were having their rag week at the time. I had quite a job collecting my ten bob until this slater fellow backed me up about the second flag.

We then came up with the idea of a dummy to look like a man hanging from the top of another chimney. Mr. Rawlinson always went home for his dinner, so I started constructing the fake corpse out of wood lathes and fencing wire. It were basically one straight stick for the backbone and a stick the other way for the arms. Coiled wire made the torso, then there were a bit of board for the pelvis with legs dangling downwards. I made the head from a sackful of old rags.

Next we had to dress this dummy, which called for all our ingenuity. My mate's wife were always going to jumble sales and she had got a monstrous overcoat which he did not like. I supplied some old pants and a pair of me father's boots filled with concrete to make the hanging look right. The body folded over at the shoulders so I could tie the whole thing in the form of a haversack.

The stack I selected was 212ft tall and situated on a road near the town centre. John Faulkner's men were working on this chimney with their red ladders all in position. Although we went there by night, all the factory lights were on and the boilers going full blast. Me mate took me as near as possible to the place, but it still meant negotiating about 24 back gardens before getting to where I wanted.

The climb were no trouble. Soon them lights were twinkling away far below me before they sort of faded. It were pitch black when I reached the staging and as I started to untie the dummy, the wind got inside it. How it ended up was quite unbelievable. Its legs were still over the shoulders while the rope for hanging it came under the crutch. Worse still the whole thing spun like a propeller.

I thought, 'This isn't going to be a success' and tried to drag it back again, fighting against the wind at 212ft. But it were no good. The dummy was being blown outwards at 45° and for a man supposed to be hanging himself it looked horrible. So I just came down that chimney, bought myself some fish and chips and went home.

The next day was a foggy Saturday with no wind. As bad luck would have it, I were working on the other side of town. I could hardly wait for 12 o'clock. The moment it was knocking off time I set off for the chimney, sort of like the crow flies. I went through gardens, across a cemetery and along the Bolton to Blackpool railway line.

When I reached the chimney area there was no sign of the hanging dummy, but groups of people stood at street corners as though there had been some sort of disaster. I said to a couple of women and a fellow,

"What's going on like?"

"Some silly sod," this fellow replied, "hung a dummy from the top of that chimney."

"Go away," I said. "What happened?"

Then the women started telling me—together. It seems that an old boy who lived on the main road across the mill woke up at first light, looked out of the window and saw the dreadful spectacle. Soon the whole neighbourhood was up and about with one person after another ringing up the police, the fire brigade and ambulances.

"The mill manager was dragged out of bed," one of the women kept saying in a knowing way. "Dragged out of bed."

"Then they dragged John Faulkner's foreman out of bed." said the other. "They knocked him up then got him down here. The police told him he would have to climb the chimney and retrieve the dead body."

Shortly afterwards, I learned, someone arrived with a pair of binoculars and those in the know realised it were a practical joke. Nevertheless John Faulkner's foreman had to bring down the dummy for analysis like. In the pocket of the jumble sale overcoat they found a Manchester bus ticket and the university students again got the blame.

The story did not quite end there. Some time later Mr. Rawlinson had me fitting a new floor in a semi near to the self-same chimney. The lady of the house was very talkative, so I asked her weren't that the stack from which the Manchester students hung a dummy? To my amazement, she broke into a hell of a frenzy.

"It may have been a dummy," she said all fierce like, "but my husband didn't know that and had a heart attack."

"A heart attack," I gulped.

"Fortunately he got over it," she continued to my relief, "but it were a bad sort of thing."

"Yes, it were," I agreed, feeling relieved. I am still a one for practical jokes, yet I never did anything like that again. Also it made me think. There I were turned twenty doing the same old joinery and gable ends for Mr. Rawlinson. True, he let me call him Bill, and I were his senior man so to speak, but I was neither a steeple jack nor my own gaffer. Whenever I spoke of this to me dad he would say,

"You're still young, Fred. Something'll turn up."

Chapter 2

False Starts

Shortly after, something did turn up. One day I found a fair sized ladder floating in our local river, which were more of an open sewer. Anyway, I fished it out, scraped it clean and painted it bright red. After pointing people's houses all day for Bill Rawlinson, I would point other people's houses in the evenings for myself. Eventually I earned £90 and bought five good ladders.

Following that it were a case of 'acquiring' pulleys and ropes. By acquiring, I mean acquiring. There was an abundance of pulley wheels left lying about half dismantled mills. As for ropes, the best source was behind Burnley Park football ground where there stood a railway goods yard and a great bridge. Kids used to take ropes from the yard to make swings under the bridge, so at nights I would take their swing ropes in turn. Lovely ropes they were with green strands running through them to prove they had come from railway company.

Around this time Bill landed a job for me at a big working mill. It meant putting in a baling press and I had the run of the place. That mill had six floors also a tower crying out to be re-pointed. One day when talking to the chief engineer I said casually like,

"Your tower needs re-pointing."

"Aye," he agreed. "I hear you do a bit of that. How much would you charge?"

I charged £140 which, looking back on it, were ridiculous. It would be more like £2,000 now. Anyway I then had to explain about only working weekends. Luckily he accepted that and I used every spare minute of my own time repointing the mill tower. It was huge though at least I could get to top through inside stairs then through a trap door.

By then Bill sort of realised there were more to my interest in steeple jacking than he had at first thought. In those days the fatality rate among steeple jacks were pretty high. Therefore whenever one fell off a chimney it was always mentioned in the papers. So Bill would cut out the article and pin it on our workshop door. Soon the door was covered with pictures and details of dead steeple jacks. He used to say it would happen to me but I am still here and he's gone.

However the job did not solve anything so far as I was concerned. I still did not know how to put ladders up a chimney. I tried talking to John Faulkner's men but they were not very bright. Most had started as labourers

the job and give me your opinion. As if you were my consultant."

I thought it were a bit unethical but, because of those planks, I did as asked. The job was a big one and in the end Mr Farnwood had me doing it with this other fellow as my assistant. I made good money on that stack, instead of being handed over to the police. With the money I bought yet more ladders.

Seeing as how my parents backyard were only 14ft square, it was getting a bit full of red ladders. They also stood halfway up the side of the house. Me father began to get a bit up tight about this perhaps because me mum could not see out of the windows. Fortunately he knew a decorator chap across the street who had a yard and we did a deal. The decorator was looking for someone to do up his premises while I wanted somewhere to put my ladders and other tackle.

Top of the Hargraves & Hamilton Ltd chimney, after treatment by Fred.

These premises were in a deplorable state of decay. The wooden fence at the front was falling down and you had to lift the gates to move them. As for the sheds, they were made out of railway sleepers and bits of old timber. I built a new brickwall along the front, re-swung the gates and sorted out everything inside for my ladders, planks, ropes, pulleys, hooks and brackets.

By that time I were both busy and beginning to make money. During the day I still worked for Bill Rawlinson. During the evenings and weekends I worked all the more for myself. The name Fred Dibnah began to be known where tough jobs were needed, particularly high up like. I began to see and plan ahead then the army caught up with me.

You see I were 22 years old and should have started my national service at 21. Bill Rawlinson tried to argue the toss on my behalf, saying I were far too valuable to go into the army. The selection board thought about this, conferred then said to Bill as if I were not there,

"We are very sorry Mr. Rawlinson, but you will have to get another operative in place of Mr. Dibnah. You see, the country is a bit hard up for men at the moment. Especially men with skills. He'll have to go."

First I had to go for a medical examination where they felt various parts of me anatomy. After that I went to some sort of careers fellow. I told him all I had done before pleading,

"Please give me a job outside like building, engineering or something of that style. If you can keep me in the open air, I'll do my national service with pleasure."

"Great," he said, "because you are going to be in a cookhouse."

So I was in the army, like it or not—but that is another story...

Once my two years was up I 'escaped' from the army. The great day came when I got on that plane which took me straight back from Germany to Manchester. I drank a bit for the first day or two after reaching home, then I went across to check my steeplejacking things in the decorators yard. The red ladders were outside, but they had been covered up and no harm came to them. The rest were in a bit of a shed, all ready to be used.

So I had cards and bill heads printed, also some photographs of jobs I had done. I was older, more experienced and able to speak for myself. I put on my best suit with a gold watch chain and set off round the mills of Bolton. Some of the chimneys looked right ropey so I was sure to find jobs. In reality, tough times lay ahead.

Chapter 3

High Climbs

While I were away feeding the troops times had gone from bad to worse in Bolton. Some of the mills shut down and the others struggled for survival. Their buildings and especially the chimneys needed repairing, but there was little or no money available. I found this out the hard way.

To begin with I did not think it best to ride a motor bike round the mills of Bolton wearing my best suit, gold watch and chain. So I used public transport which restricted me to less calls per day. Then, when I got there, they would keep me sitting in the foyer for an hour or more before telling me my services were not required.

Nowadays I go straight into the managing director or chief engineer being more well known like, but I have never fogotten those unhappy days of having to wait for nothing. In fact I had some right rebuffs when I came out of the army and was looking for steeplejack work. After several weeks it began to seem as if I were getting nowhere fast. So for two or three days at a time, I would do odd jobs for local property repairers. You know—a slate on here for Mr. Smith and a new bit of guttering for Mrs. Brown.

Out of the money earned this way, I would give me mum a regular sum for supporting me while the rest generally went on fags and the odd pint. This went on for over six months. Always, after three days repairing, I would go round the mills again for a couple of days. I was after real chimney work but during that time I never got a single stack to mend.

At long last I had a slight stroke of luck. There were then three breweries in Bolton, one of them near the art school. The owner's house was next door and I had been quite friendly with his son when we were lads. By now the son had become a man and he worked in the family brewery whose chimney were in a diabolical condition.

Partly because of our old aquaintanceship, but mostly because something had to be done about that stack before it fell down, I was given the job. I shall never forget the first chimney I ever mended. I spent three weeks making everything perfect for which I earned £45. While doing so, I did not know where the next job was coming from.

Anyway the brewery stack needed a new metal band round the top and me father introduced me to a welder-cum-metalwork fellow. I talked to this chap quite a bit as he was making the band which fitted fine. After finishing the brewery job, I began searching for more work and thought I would look in to see the welder fellow.

"I'm glad you called." he said. "The vicar of Bolton wants to see you."
"What for?" I asked.
"Best go and talk to him yourself," he replied.
Here I should say a little about that vicar who was a funny sort of fellow. He was a good Christian mind, which can be strange to some clergymen, but he had a mad look about him. At that time he drove a huge black 1929 Humber limousine with a bonnet about six feet long. Anyway, I zoomed off to see him on me 1927 AJS which he thought were marvellous, so I used it more and more after that.
"Ah yes," he said at last when I managed to bring up the matter of work, "I want you to take a squint at my weathervane." We then both looked upwards as if to Heaven.

Early days with a younger Fred on his marvellous 1927 AJS motor bike. Even then the flat cap and cigarette were very much part of Fred's 'image'.

If you have ever been to Bolton, you will know that the church tower is the tallest thing in town. From the ground the vane looks like a postage stamp. Actually the main bit is 6ft 6in long and 3ft deep-as big as a back door—and made of heavy metal. How them Victorians manhandled it up there in the first place I shall never know. It were going to be bad enough job just repairing it.

To begin with the task seemed impossible. Fortunately I was able to get most of the way up the tower by a staircase in the middle. This came out level with four pinnacles and from there I had to stick up me red ladders then put scaffold round them. The view from the top was fantastic. It seemed more like 10 miles high than 200ft.

After I had seen to the weathervane, the vicar wanted it gilded all over. This meant putting on gold leaf, not the easiest of jobs at that height on a windy day. Anyway I did what was required and, apart from getting my picture in the local rag, which did me a bit of good, this chief vicar chap put a word round the other Bolton clergy.

The massive weather van at the top of the spire of Bolton Parish Church, following repair and gilding.

As I said, he was a bit of a character. Among his many interests he liked firearms. He and I used to sit in the cemetery with him telling me about all the lethal weapons he possessed. Once, when I could get a word in, I mentioned that I had sort of come back from Germany with a Luger pistol. Immediately the mad look came into his eyes. He had to have one—preferably mine.

I thought it would blow over but the next time we met in the graveyard, the vicar revealed to me he had his own firing range up on the moors.

"Whenever I feel like a shoot out," he said with that look of his, "I pack the Humber with my whole armoury in proper Al Capone style." I doubt if he had firearm certificates for half his guns, not bothering much about paperwork as he told me. So I hoped the subject would be dropped. However the third time we happened to meet in the cemetery the vicar said excitedly,

"I'm going up on the moors next Wednesday. To have a good blaze away. Care to join me? You could bring that Luger with you."

He would not take no for an answer and it seemed the solution to another problem. You see, me mum did not like the gun—any gun— and she had locked it up in her parlour cupboard. Well on the Wednesday while she was out at work, the Vicar of Bolton and I arrived outside the house in his black limousine.

Of course I had a key for the front door but we could not find the key for that parlour cupboard. Hunt high and low we did, with him getting wilder as time went on. In the end we had to kind of burgle the cupboard. I was not too keen about it. However the vicar just had to have that Luger.

The story did not end there though. After we had fired everything on the moors and returned to town, the vicar suddenly remembered another appointment.

"Have to visit some parish ladies," he told me. "Would you be a good chap and put my guns in the vestry?'

I had to walk about 200 yards to the church and, as luck would have it, the council just happened to be knocking down the Grand Theatre at the time. All the roads were blocked and there were policemen officiating everywhere. To get to the vestry, I had to talk my way past one policeman after another, pretending I were carrying the tools of me trade.

But that vicar was a good friend as I said. He got me my next job mending the clock faces on another church tower. Everything I touched up there came away in my hands and it ended up with some major reconstruction.

For example, on top of that church spire there was a huge iron rod, on which the weather vane was mounted, also a monstrous bolt with a proper head at one end leading through to a nut and washer at the other. If you look up slender church spires and wonder how the weathervane does not blow off, it is because of that rod up the middle, also the giant nut, bolt and washer.

Trouble is they were all put up and forgotten over hundred years ago, with the weather helping the rust on ever since. By the time I got there, that bolt was no thicker than a ball point pen. The job sticks in my mind because it were the first of its kind I had to do. I also kept taking photographs and putting them in me work album which had 'F. Dibnah Steeplejack' gold embossed on the front.

But mending church steeples was not the same as working on industrial chimneys. So one day I summoned up enough courage to visit the biggest firm in the area—Dick Hargraves. It was a very forbidding sort of place with iron pillars, iron door and an iron portcullis type of gate. At 5.30 everyone used to come out of there as if they had been in prison all day.

It was a fine day and I decided to go on my motor bike, which was sort of impressive with carbide lamps and a great bull horn. As luck would have it, I roared into the place and very nearly knocked over the boss man. Fortunately he showed more interest in me bike than the photo album I had strapped on to a back bracket.

Next thing he were saying if I had a moment or two he would take me round his works and show me all the chimneys. It was full of them, most built in the 1860's. I found a big opening there and have had a more or less permanent arrangement with them ever since. The money I made on their first job enabled me to buy 10 more ladders making 30 in all.

Up to then I did everything sort of single-handed which made the hard work all the harder. So I began to look for an assistant and latched on to an old fellow called Percy Porter. I taught him how to tie knots and handle the equipment, then we went out to tackle a 200ft chimney. Percy is still with me. Lives down the road in a bungalow.

Shortly after Percy joined me, I were summoned to an unbelievable chimney 270ft high. I had just enough ladders to go up it, but nowhere near enough scaffolding to go round the top. The engineer told me they wanted the top half off the stack, as it was surplus to requirements and a liability stuck so far up in the sky. Besides they had to pay heavy insurance for the thing.

When I reached the top I found a length of railway line the old timers had used. It were like a beam across the centre for pulling up materials. They had

Bolton Parish Church, November 1963. Work included pointing and long-overdue attention to the weather vane.

moved this beam higher and higher when the chimney was being built. Then, on reaching the top, they left it there. Now I had to get it down again.

The length of railway line was too heavy to manhandle, so I set about cutting it in half with a hacksaw. The top half had acquired like a hard skin on it and I used seven blades just getting through this. After that it were not too bad, though I had to give up sitting on the rail as I sawed away towards the end.

There was a bit of spare ground by the foot of the chimney and Percy warned everyone to keep out of the area. The first piece I threw down landed horizontally while the second went in end on. They both disappeared completely and for all I know are still there.

Anyway I began taking the chimney down brick by brick Apart from the hard graft, this operation was made all the more difficult by the smoke billowing out all the time. You see they could not stop production and, one way or another, it took me six months. Some nights I went home looking like a smoked kipper.

As I bashed away at each brick with my hammer and chisel, I used to think about our ancesters who put up all those mill houses and chimneys. They were sort of building their own pyramids and they did so in style. No one takes much notice of what they did nowadays, but I have had close-ups of beautiful stone dressings and magnificent brick formations.

Another bonus was the view one got from the top of a 200ft chimney especially during the winter. There would be those endless rows of Coronation Street terraced houses, each puffing out smoke to add to that of the big factory stacks. All the smoke would combine to form layers through which the winter sun filtered—grey pink in the mornings and deep purple just before nightfall.

In addition to Percy Porter, I took on another man called Joe Robinson. Joe was very strong even when nudging 70 and was of great help to me until he died recently. I remember one morning, he and me arriving at a stack. There were a real pea soup fog on and we could not see very far up the side.

"You're not going up there," said Joe, "to throw things down today?" He said it as if I was a bit crazy.

"Course I am," I said. "Work must go on. So you rope off a landing area in case any fool walks into the firing line."

Well up there it was like being in an aeroplane above the clouds. The sun was bright and beautiful, which made me kind of carefree. I started slinging bricks off but forgot that while doing this, I were working my way round the chimney stack. Before long, I were well away from the roped off landing area.

It began to dawn on me that when I threw a brick down, a different sort of noise came up through the fog. So I chucked another in the same direction and the sound of breaking slate or glass reached my ears. Next thing there were shouts from below like 'Oy!'. Then I remembered that on the opposite side of the chimney from my landing area for bricks there stood a rather splendid office.

It had a slate roof, plenty of big glass windows and a fancy plastered ceiling. Below that came the walnut panelling and what they called their 'terrazzo hallway'. But I was worried more about killing somebody as I went down the ladders three rungs at a time.

When I reached the ground and looked towards the building it was to see everyone cowering in a doorway. They were all covered in plaster from the owner of the place downwards. No one said a word to me as I wandered into the terrazzo hallway and up to their once magnificent office.

The first sight I came across were some cornice mouldings about a foot thick laying beside the door. Beyond it lay layer upon layer of roof plaster into which fair-sized chimney bricks stuck out like they had been dive bombers. The desks, typewriters and even the tea cups had been properly peppered.

Everyone was so relieved to have escaped loss of life or limb, they treated it like some great adventure. I was glad to go along with that and, in the end, help to repair the roof. Years later I had to remove the rest of the chimney and I wandered into the office to bring back the memory like. The evidence were all there if you knew where to look and people talked excitedly to me about it—as if they had been in the Battle of the Somme.

After that I became very safety conscious, not only for myself but on account of others. I kept a lookout for dangerous chimneys and could spot them a mile off. There was a stack I remember above a warehouse sort of place where I went to buy a replacement cupboard for the one me mum kept complaining had been wrecked in getting the Luger pistol out. An old colliery originally occupied the site and the chimney stood over the unused engine house.

This stack were in a terrible shape as I noted on entering the yard. So I bought the cupboard—all smiles there—then I suggested putting right their chimney. Even when I brought along my photo album, to show I were genuine like, the warehouse fellow was not convinced.

"Look." I argued, "that iron ring round the top is hardly holding itself together let alone the chimney. See how those bricks are bulging. There's a lot of pressure behind them. All you need is a change in temperature and bang-crash. It will come down like one of those medieval things them knights used in battle.''

''You're trying to frighten me.'' the fellow said, ''but I'm not at all scared.''

''Be it on your own head then.'' I said and meant it.

A few days later there was frantic knocking on our front door. Outside was this warehouse fellow who told me he had a problem.

''What sort of problem?...'' I began to ask when he said,

''It's that chimney Bits are beginning to fall off it.''

Well I were round there quicker than he was. When I arrived at the warehouse, the place was swarming with police and building inspectors. As usual, when anything falls off a chimney, everyone panics. The fellow was white about the gills yet in a way he were a lucky man.

Luckily for him the piece of stack fell away from an adjoining house. If it had come down on the other side of the chimney, the bit would have gone straight through the house—both floors. There had been a girl asleep in the top room and people downstairs. As I said, the warehouse fellow were lucky and he changed his tune completely.

''How much will you charge to do it for me?'' he asked, then proceeded knocking me down to a rock-bottom price.

But the job had to be done and I did it. I took the top 6ft off the chimney, put a new iron band round and pointed 10ft downwards. Finally, just before I was ready to remove my ladders, this warehouse fellow said to me,

''I have had some company namesigns prepared. I want you to fix them up there. Right at the top so everyone can see them.''

I tried explaining to him that you are not supposed to put up business signs without permission, but he replied,

''If you want me to pay you, you'll do as I say.''

So I did, with one of his signs facing the town hall. After that I whipped my ladders away.

It were not many hours before he phoned me. The town hall had been on to him saying his signs were illegal and must come down immediately. Right, I told him, but it will be another job. Right, he agreed between his teeth. He did not want the signs and I used the wood from them to make more kitchen cupboards and placate me mum.

Here I should explain that steeplejacking can be like a bug that bites you. When I was working on the warehouse chimney, a young fellow kept hanging round. We got talking and I could see he was bitten by the bug despite him being a violinist in the Halle Orchestra—in the front row so he must have been good. His name was Kenneth.

After the warehouse job, which were fiddling to me, I had to take down a massive 200ft chimney for Courtaulds. It was going to be a big task and, when he heard of it, Kenneth asked if he could assist like. Instead of practising for some concert in the Free Trade Hall, he came and helped me ladder that chimney to the very top.

We managed to knock the top 40-50ft off the chimney, then things became difficult. Some bricks were hard and others soft, the same for the mortar, but nothing would break away easily. Those old chimney builders must have known a trick or two that I did not know. Kenneth was as intrigued as me in cracking the job and neglected his violin practice all the more.

One of the things we thought of was to take a road drill up there. It were a bit precarious like but we had a go. That did not work either. When we put the bit of the drill into the bricks, it just bored a hole yet nothing would come away. Another problem was I had not quoted enough for the job and the weeks were going by.

Kenneth the violinist and I thought of everything. We thought of a few 'poppers' but Courtaulds did not want explosives. We devised some incredible mechanical contraptions, with screw jacks and still that chimney held together. We then used a 50 ton hydraulic jack in another fantastic contraption. After that we worked inside the chimney chiselling away the entire bottom lining.

Then all of a sudden came disaster. The chimney, which had been so stubborn, decided to split right down the middle. One piece about 4ft square went down its centre. Another piece, twice as big bounced off the side and went through the roof of Courtauld's blacksmith's shops, hitting the main shaft which drove all their machinery. As I said to Kenneth the violinist,

"At least you have a job with the Halle. My steeplejacking career seems to have come to an end."

While this disaster were taking place, the chief engineer was playing billards in the canteen at the other end of the works, it being their dinner hour. One of the lads raced across to the canteen and broke the news in blunt North of England style.

"Fred's just wrecked the blacksmith's shop."

Luckily for me this chief engineer were a Sir Francis Drake type—you know, the one who played bowls while Armada sailed up Channel.

"Anyone killed?" he asked still squinting along his cue.

"No sir."

"Oh well, I'd best finish off this game."

That chimney resisted me until the end. Apart from the 50 ton jack, I took a steam roller to it, then pulled off lumps with a wire halter. When it were over Kenneth the violinist and I went into a pub and got drunk. Maybe it was the drink, but I fancied the ghosts of the Victorian men who built that stack were laughing at me.

The offending piece of brickwork, supported by a hydraulic jack at Courtauld's Caleb Wright Mill, Tyldsley. Not long after this photograph was taken it was on the ground—in the blacksmith's shop!

Chapter 4

Me Marriage

I first saw Alison when she was only 13. I were working on her father's roof at the time and her being about the place sort of distracted me. That time I made the mistake of asking her dad if I could go out with her. Being a man of few words he simply said. "Keep away, son". Which I had to do.

However I kept an eye on Alison in a proprietary sort of way. The years went by with my climbing the ladder so to speak. Then one evening who should come into our local but her—again with her dad. This time I tried to butter him up a bit but he still did not like me, perhaps on account of my life style.

However, I managed to talk to Alison quite a bit on such interesting subjects as chimney stacks and steam engines. She had grown up and filled out quite a bit, also she was more independent of her father since we last met. After a pint or two, to summon up some Dutch courage, I asked her if she fancied coming out with me and that was how it all began.

As you might say we started courting and, after a few weeks of that, we decided to become engaged. We went to a jeweller I knew and bought the ring. From then on it became official like.

Another month or two went by during which plans began to be drawn up by just about everyone else for our wedding. Also my pals who never thought I would ever wed anybody, pulled my leg something terrible. There was so much fuss that I suggested to Alison we go off and leave the lot of them.

She wondered where we could go, which indicated she might be interested, and I told her about a mate of mine. He had landed a fantastic job in Scotland as chauffeur to a lady owning a big house and estate. He kept letting me know there was plenty of room and I could visit him at anytime.

"Bring anyone you like," he said. "It is very free and easy here, open house and all that."

When Alison agreed I rushed home, packed a bag and hid it in my workshop. I also collected some cash from a recent job which had been stached for such a purpose. Came the cold light of dawn and I began wondering if Alison would show up at the railway station where we agreed to meet. She did and after that there were no turning back.

We took a train which went to Carlisle. 'Gateway to Scotland' the railway posters said with a fancy picture in the hopes of people going there.

But there were not many people on the train and those that were kept getting out. In the end we were left with one posh looking man sat in the corner opposite us.

He was reading a magazine while we were full of what we had done and sort of wanted to share the news. So after a while I managed to engage the man in conversation. Eventually I was able to tell him we had got around to running away from both our families, to do things our own way, to which he said,

"Oh, bloody good show."

After that he got out as well.

From Carlisle, which looked nothing like the fancy poster, we had to catch a series of buses that took us across the border into Scotland, then westwards to my mate in Kirkudbrightshire. The Scottish scenery and our bus journey seemed to go on forever. By the time we reached Dumfries, I was becoming a bit unsure of where exactly my mate worked. Alison was getting a bit quiet as well but she said,

"You'll have to ask."

I decide to ask at Dumfries bus station. It were a huge place with a long line of Leyland single deckers. One chap looked knowledgeable so I went up and acquainted him of our situation. To begin with he acted as puzzled as I was, then he suggested trying someone called Angus.

"Oh aye, Angus," he kept saying. "See the last bus at the other end of the line. Angus drives that. I should try him if I were you."

The bus was ticking over when we arrived there with Angus already in the driving seat. He and the passengers listened with impassive faces as I went into another long explanation. It seemed I was not getting through when Angus suddenly said,

'Oh aye, I've heard of the Sassenach chauffeur. Get on my bus and I'll take you to him."

Naturally we thought this an incredible stroke of luck. We were on target again so to speak. Alison and I put our bags on the racks, sat down and nodded in our friendly Lancashire way at the passengers who continued to stare impassively back at us.

Anyway Angus the driver proceeded to take us across country that looked as if it had come from another planet. There were not a house to be seen, bleak moors every where and of course it started to rain. Even so people kept getting out and disappearing into the mist. Then, when we were in the middle of nowhere, Angus stopped the bus and called to us,

"This is where you get out for your Sassenach chauffer."

"You have to be joking," I said though he did not look that sort of chap. "There's nothing here."

"Oh aye there is," he corrected me. "See that track leading through the pine forest and away up yon mountain. You'll find your friend up there."

It were unbelievable and we acted in a sort of daze. We took down our bags, left the bus and a moment later it too disappeared in the pouring rain. Alison was none too happy about the way things were turning out and neither was I. There was nothing else we could do but press on, which is what we did.

We walked and we walked, getting wetter and wetter, but saw nothing but trees and moorland. As we got higher up the mountain, wind joined the rain in attacking us. Just when it all seemed hopeless an estate car with two ladies in it appeared beside us. The ladies looked like mother and daughter, which they were. They eyed us up and down through the car windows while we just stood there. Eventually the mother lowered her window, gave us a closer look, then announced,

"This is private land."

In normal circumstance I would have been tempted to tell her what to do with her private land. However this seemed the time to act a bit humble-like, so I explained who we were and why we happened to be climbing a mountain in a rain storm. When I got to the bit about my mate from Bolton, who had come to these parts as a chauffeur, the mother said,

"You'd best get in the back."

So we stowed our cases, then sat down wet and dripping while the car continued up the mountain. Eventually, when we were just below the clouds, we came to this jolly Scottish farm surrounded by fertile fields of gorse, bracken and big boulders. The sheep looked at us sort of pityingly and the farmer was just the same.

At least they had a good fire going and over a cup of tea we listened to a long yarn about the estate being split up and the changes that had taken place. Alison was sort of silent by now so I had to get the matter settled, having talked her into this elopement business.

"But my mate," I interrupted, "who was the chauffeur. Do you know where I can find him?"

"Oh aye," they said, "he went to a place called Bolton."

As there were no more buses that day and the sun had given up as well, we were invited to stay the night. As you can imagine it was kind of different to what we had planned. Alison was led away to what looked like a cot set in a wall, while I had to sleep with the farmer who wore a night shirt, also a cap with a bobble on the end.

As soon as dawn arrived the family were out and about in oilskins and gumboots trying to find their cows. This gave Alison and I an opportunity to have a talk. At first we did not know what to do. To return to Bolton would mean losing face. In the end we decided on Plan B. We would go and get married at Gretna Green, which we had passed on our way into Scotland.

This meant another car journey down the mountain, then waiting for a bus where the track met the main road. At least it was not raining and our spirits rose a bit. We would be wed in Gretna, all brisk like, before continuing to Bolton where we would have something to tell them.

At Gretna Green, the registry office told us we would have to stay there 21 days before we could be married. This was a serious blow because my money was fast running out. To make matters a bit more difficult Alison said she did not fancy a registry office wedding on its own. She wanted a church one as well.

Fortunately I am a resourceful sort of chap. I noticed that the gable ends of most buildings needed re-pointing, beginning with the hotel where we would have to stay. So I put it to the manager. Being Scottish, he haggled a bit but I could hold my own coming from Lancashire. He also told me where the minister lived so I could solve Alison's problem as well.

Unfortunately that minister was not at all keen.

"I'm afraid," he said putting the tips of his fingers together, "I do not take kindly to couples who run away from their homes. Nothing personal mind, but there it is."

The situation was becoming tricky again. Alison had started it in the first place so I held back to see if she could cope. I must say she did her pleading bit very well, but the minister was firm with her.

"I am not at all keen." He was tapping his fingertips now. "Not at all keen."

While this was going on, I had a look about the room. Over the mantlepiece hung a magnificent picture of the Forth Bridge. I said how much I admired it and swung the conversation round to working at great heights. I only did chimneys, I said modestly, but the Forth Bridge, that was something else.

"Oh aye." said the minister, "Scottish built."

"Fantastic!" I agreed.

He told me all about it and I listened intently. At last he sort of came round to our particular problem.

"Well," he said, "if you stayed the stipulated three weeks I might see my way to marrying you. Do I hear tell you re-point gable ends?"

So we stayed on somehow and the three weeks went by. On the day before we were due to be married in the registry office I alerted the minister.

"Oh aye, just come round afterwards, knock on the door and I'll perform the ceremony."

Which is what we did. It was quite late in the morning and there was Alison and I knocking on his door in turn. At last we heard this shuffling inside the house and the minister appeared in his pyjamas. Was his face red when he saw us.

"I had forgotten about you." he admitted. "Clean forgotten."

"Is it alright?" I asked knowing Alison had set her heart on him marrying us.

"Of course." he replied. "Just give me a minute."

He shut the door and scarcely a minute later reappeared in a cassock —over his pyjamas. So Alison had her church wedding and could return to Bolton with a clear conscience. There was a lot of talk of course with folk whispering, "Just like Fred" or "Poor Alison" but we are still together, which is more than you can say for a lot of fancy weddings.

Aveling & Porter steam roller 'Alison' (prior to fitting of canopy), in Radcliffe Road, outside the Dibnah's house. This has been restored from a derelict state, having originally been a Victorian gatehouse building.

During the next few months Alison and I lived with me parents. That is never any good, yet somehow we all made it work. She and I looked at one place after another but there was always a problem. Then one day the Earl of Bradford's agent Stanley Boardman, who I had worked for many a time, rang asking me to step over to his office. I thought it were going to be another job until he said,

"Fred, we have a bit of property that might interest you and Mrs Dibnah. As a family house if you take my meaning."

"What and where is it?" I asked.

"It was a Victorian gatehouse," he replied, "and it is just off Radcliffe Road."

"Hey." I said, "that's a bit of a posh district."

"Well the place needs doing up." he admitted, "and I thought what with your capabilities....."

"We'll have a look at it." I said.

Mr. Boardman took us there himself. It were a fair sized place, which we wanted, but he had been right about the repairs. The old gate house was beginning to stick out like a sore thumb in that good, quiet residential district.

"We'll take it," I said, "on one condition."

"Which is?" asked the Earl of Bedford's agent.

"I can bring my steam roller up here."

"Oh Fred..." Alison began, being worried about me upsetting the neighbourhood from the start. However I were firm even though it meant having to cut a new approach road round the quiet hillside. That was how we got the house we still live in today. I like to stick to priorities in life.

Now you may well ask what Alison felt about my activities of steeple jacking and working on me steam engines. The truth is she went along with both of them. In the case of my having to work at great heights, she realised I was a professional always keeping within safety margins as I shall describe later in this book. In fact the only ladder I have ever fallen off was a stepladder when decorating a room. It were ridiculous but she has never stopped reminding me of it. As for steam engines, well Alison reckons with female logic it keeps me nearby instead of down the pub.

Anyway there we were with our own place which had to be repaired, redecorated and furnished. Typically it came at a time when I were short of work and money. The winter months especially were hard with jobs difficult to come by. During such times you discover who your real friends are, also how lucky you are having a wife willing to take the rough with the rough.

There are not many wives who will put in a day's labouring mixing mortar and carrying hods of bricks. To reward her I used to let her light the fires under chimneys that had to come down. It became a sort of tradition with us like and to this day that is a job she never misses. Alison also helped me with the books and even debt collecting.

The chimney repair and demolition business is a peculiar one as I must explain. You see people like so-called property developers would buy up old mills and rent them out to other businesses. Generally no one gave a thought for the chimney stacks still stuck up there. That is, until one of them chimneys began falling apart and becoming a liability.

Now this particular chimney was beside a mill belonging to a property company headed by a Jewish gentleman. I had heard that none of the other steeple jacks would look at the stack, let alone climb up it. That chimney were a nasty one and the man who took on the job, they kept saying, would end up dead.

On the other hand the offer being made by this Jewish gentleman kept inching up. He liked to handle everything to do with money even if it meant negotiating with mere steeple jacks. So there was this sort of waiting game going on with the chimney crumbling, the other jacks saying no and the property developer raising the ready.

Apart from the money, which I desperately needed, that stack presented a challenge to me. If I could demolish it, my reputation would rise with my bank balance. I talked it over with Alison and she said you can do it.

But first I had to negotiate with the Jewish gentleman. He was most courteous and listed his conditions in the clearest of terms. If I felled the chimney without damaging any of his property, let alone maiming or killing somebody, he would pay me the agreed sum within one month. Knowing him, I insisted on everything in writing to which he readily agreed.

Though I say so myself, I did a perfect job. Text book you might say if there were any books about taking down chimneys. Even the Jewish gentleman, who came to inspect the job, agreed it could not be bettered. He seemed very interested in my line of work, continued to talk to me most courteous like and ended up by assuring me,

"I'll pay you within the month as agreed."

Fifteen months later he still had not paid me.

Now I can usually look after myself, including getting the money owed to me, but in this case I were stumped every way. If I went to the property developer's office, the bird in the front hall would look right through me while suggesting it was usual to write or ring. When I wrote—and I certainly gnawed the tops off many ball point pens—my letters went unanswered. When I phoned, it was to get on to some underling who said he would look into it, ring me back but never did.

In vain I tried to get through to the Jewish gentleman. He was either off doing a deal in another part of the world or, more usually, at a meeting. His

Alison Dibnah strikes the match to light the fire under a chimney, this having become a family tradition.

secretaries called them conferences. He seemed to have hundreds of them. At times I would get very stroppy, then some smooth talking fellow would come on the phone and end up by assuring me the cheque was going into the post. He would do it himself. That very day. Rest assured Mr.... what did you say your name was?

But the cheque never came. However what was coming happened to be Christmas with Alison talking about extra expenses and hinting about me giving her a present. There was also my steam roller, needing several vital parts, so I began to get worried. What could I do?

"What can I do?" I said one morning at breakfast.

"You can let me collect the money," said Alison, "in my own way."

"What way is that?" I asked, more cautious like.

"Never you mind." she said. "Only, if I am not back by this evening, will you tell the local papers?"

That got me proper worried and I became more concerned when she informed me of her fee for collecting that debt. Of all things, Alison wanted a new dress which, considering we had been married some time, was to my mind a bit pushy.

Anyway off she went impetuous like and halfway through the afternoon turned up with the cheque. I was just in time to bank it and to my delight, it did not bounce. Then Alison told me how she had managed to succeed

Fred with one of the two Alisons in his life...

where I had failed.

To start with she would have no truck with the cool looking bird at the front desk. In fact the lady was sent upstairs with the message that Mrs Dibnah intended to sit in the hall, like forever, until the money owing us for 15 months were paid.

Apparently dozens of people came to look at her—from office boys and little dolly typists, to managers, executives and others of that ilk. They came all the way from their palatial offices on the upper floors. They tried to reason with her and left her waiting through their dinner hour, but Alison sat on. Eventually after trying the "It will be in the post" trick, a senior partner brought the signed cheque down to her. She never did see the Jewish gentleman, but there was no doubt weeping and gnashing of teeth on the top story.

I do not wish to give the impression that I am against the Chosen Race. In fact they are as generous as drunken sailors when compared to some of the Lancashire mill owners I have known. While haggling with one such character in his walnut panelled office, I found myself out of cigarettes. Still haggling he crossed the carpet to a big green corner safe with very impressive brass handles on it. Producing a set of keys he opened three locks, then took out a packet of ten. He gave me one, returned the packet carefully to the safe, relocked it, pocketed the keys and went on telling me why he had to pay me so little for risking my life. It were unbelievable.

But to get back to me marriage. Alison and I were blessed, as the local vicar put it, with three daughters. They are Jayne, Lorna and little Caroline. You will appreciate that they make up a gang of four females when joined by their mother. They expect to eat, to be clothed and even to go on holidays. We have had some ghastly experiences such as at Blackpool, though I managed to get round the scrap yards and helped out on a few gable ends with Alison mixing and handing up the cement.

The latest problem is a picture of me in the front parlour before which they all bow down whenever I try to apply fatherly discipline. To help family relations along like, I named my favourite 13 ton steam roller after Alison. In my opinion you cannot say fairer than that.

Chapter 5

Odd Jobs

The nearest I have ever come to death, funny as it may seem, was not up a chimney but down a hole in the ground. An estate agent I knew lived in the country and he had an old well in his garden which worried him. There were two big flagstones over the top, with a crack down the middle and my friend wanted me to find out how deep the well was and if it were dangerous.

I lay squinting between the flagstones, then set fire to pages of the Financial Times and watched them burning until they reached the bottom. This seemed to be 40-50 feet down, quite dry and might have been a mineshaft. I made enquiries and learned there were very early types of coal mines in my friend's part of the country. Anyway I left it at that because the flagstones seemed to be enormous.

However the estate agent was still worried about such a great hole on his property. To begin with, cars had to drive across these flagstones, also he had a great traction engine which went quite close to the side. One winter's morning he found where I was working and came to see me.

"Fred." he said, "I must have that well or mine shaft seen to. Repaired or filled in. It's bothering me. Next thing you know there'll be an accident."

I said I would do it, little knowing that I would be the victim.

Well the agreed date arrived. Together with Donald my assistant at the time, we loaded up the van and set out to the estate agent's place. Our first task was to remove those flagstones which proved even harder than I imagined, being about 8 ft long by 4 ft across and over 3 ins in thickness. It took time and effort to lift those flags, then move them out of the road.

Now we could look down the shaft and what we saw proved more peculiar still. For the first 15 ft or so, the sides were lined with bricks but not as we know them. These bricks were about 2 ins thick and had been laid without mortar. After that came rock faces with bits of rotten timber sticking out here and there. All in all, it looked rather dangerous and unhealthy.

The next thing we did was to put two long scaffolding pipes across the top from which Donald could lower me in my bosun's chair. This preliminary inspection clearly showed that many of the lower bricks were falling away. It seemed to me that we could undermine the bad areas, put a proper footing in the rock face, then make good the missing bricks.

In order to get 15 ft down, we suspended four more scaffolding poles from the crosspieces and fitted smaller ones below to hold a working platform. At the beginning everything went to plan. We repaired one area and started on another. Then I became inquisitive to see what lay at the bottom of that well or mineshaft. There might, I thought, be interesting tunnels leading off it.

I also thought the bosun's chair would be perfectly safe. It had carried me up and down many a chimney and it would take more than my weight to break the ropes. So telling Donald what I was doing, I began to lower myself slowly and cautiously.

When I was about 3 ft from what looked like the bottom, bits and pieces of bricks began to fall around me, some hitting my flat cap. At the same time, Donald's voice echoed down to me.

"You'd better come up Fred. Summat seems wrong."

By then the lumps were getting bigger and had me worried. Something was really wrong, but I still had no idea of the real danger. Nevertheless I do not think any man ever went up vertically quicker in a bosun's chair than in the whole history of bosun's chairs! I was up to the top in no time and Donald pulled me away from that strange hole in the ground.

We waited for a bit, looking this way and that, but nothing more happened. Thinking it were a false alarm, I went down to the working platform 15 ft below the surface. Donald then handed me my brick laying equipment before fetching a load of bricks. While he was getting them, I decided to knock a bit of broken brick out of the ancient wall. I gave it a preliminary tap like and, all of a sudden, the wall began groaning.

You get a feeling about these things. I though something is seriously wrong and I must get out of here. At the same time I remember thinking that I must also take my trowel and spirit level with me. It is strange how your mind works in an emergency. However I was up and over the top a split second before everything else started to slide down the hole.

I mean everything. All the old bricks went, the platform I had been standing on was smashed to bits and those extra strong scaffolding poles were bent like paperclips. Even the two pipes across the top were taken some 40-50 feet down the shaft before jamming themselves between the rock faces.

The whole episode were a bit of a horror really but we had not come to the end of it. What I had thought was the bottom had been a piece of wood with so much debris to ressemble a firm dry surface. The weight of bricks cleared all that away and plunged a further 70 ft to black water. I am not a swimmer so, if the fall of rocks had not brained me, I would have drowned down there.

You might think Donald and I had had enough. To us however that accident was a stroke of luck. The fall of old bricks cleanly cleared away the entire rock faces. We used about 5,000 new bricks in their place, nice and solid all the way round. We then fitted two big iron girders across which could take the weight of a Centurian tank, before putting the flagstones back in position. You would never know they had been moved yet they were—as I have related—and brought me the nearest I have come to death.

Death and danger are things you live with as a steeple jack, also you see them from new angles. This is very noticeable when working on church steeples above grave yards. Many a time I have looked straight down on such places all empty and desolate. Then more often than you would imagine a cortege pulls up with the hearse in front and just one car behind.

I always stop working at such times to pay my respects to the departed. Whenever I see just the vicar in front and the widow behind, with not a single friend following, I wonder what the fellow had been like. At other times, I see these little coffins, barely a foot long and six inches wide. They are generally planted across the end of some other grave that nobody knows about. Soon the grass grows over them and both look lonely from where I am watching 200 ft above the ground.

Working on churches puts you in touch with all sorts of other people. On one occasion I met a travelling grave digger who had an old car and a stack of new shovels. He told me about his trade and I happened to mention that I was trying to set up a blacksmith's shop but needed an anvil. As luck would have it, the grave digger said he knew of an anvil which had been thrown away about 10 years ago.

It turned out that a lot of broken stones had also been thrown over the anvil and it would need digging out. This grave digger said he had hurt his back but, if I could help him dig a few graves, he would in turn help me to recover the anvil. So I ended up being an amateur and part time grave digger myself.

The first grave I ever dug gave me several problems. There needs to be quite a depth to a grave—say 6 feet or more—but by the time you get to 4-5 ft down it is difficult to throw out the shovelfuls of clay. They begin to tumble back and you get to thinking about being buried yourself. The trick is to leave a hump in the middle and take it out last.

Anyway I was digging this grave in what I thought was virgin soil when the shovel struck something hard. That's strange I thought, then the next stroke took the shovel head across the top of a coffin, which could not have been there long because there was a cross on it. At least there was, until my shovel sheared the four screws holding it down and the cross sort of jumped up at me.

I froze and looking down saw there were a big crack right along the middle of the lid, which went inwards, and a large knot hole which definitely had space below it. I had not reckoned on a Count Dracula job so I was out of that hole smartish and went to my grave digger friend for advice.

"Often happens," he told me, "in this business. You'll have to fill it in again I'm afraid and start somewhere else."

Even when the grave digger's back was better and he had helped me get my anvil, we continued to do mutual business. It worked this way. He would dig the grave and I would fill it in after the ceremony. This meant he could take on more jobs while it was extra cash for me.

"Right Fred," he would say, "there's a grave dug in such-and-such a churchyard and the funeral will be over by 2.30. I'll leave a spare shovel in the boiler house."

The aerial view of the graveyard from the tower of St. Stephens & All Saints, Lever Bridge in 1966—note the temporary 2ft gauge railway on the left.

Narrow gauge wagon on Fred's Graveyard Railway, used for the transport of materials during the dismantling of the church tower.

I learned that church boiler houses were the favourite place for grave diggers to leave their shovels, also there were other tricks to the trade. For example, grave diggers sometimes cheated on the depth of the holes, but always left the earth looking piled up high with a bit of imitation grass over the top.

Anyway I would nip down from whatever steeple I were mending in the vicinity. As I said it brought in a few more quid. However the rather shallow graves left by my digger began to be criticised by undertakers and I started to get the blame. Not that undertakers were blameless themselves. Theirs was also a peculiar trade.

There was one fellow I knew who ran a collection of very large, muscle-bound assistants who swore profusely, played cards every dinner time and lost all their wages to him. They would look quiet and humble like on duty but a moment later were drinking and smoking again with great gusto.

Anyway this head chap said he would show me inside a crematorium-you know, what goes on behind them purple curtians. Up to then, like most other people, I had heard unbelievable tales of coffins not being burnt, then sold again and again to other bereaved relatives. Well that is all rubbish. Basically what happens is this.

After the deceased has rolled away to a nice gentle tune on the organ, the coffin with him in it is put on what resembles a huge iron trolley, something like the one used for operations in hospitals. The coffin and deceased are then wheeled into the furnace which works off gas and compressed air. It looks like a baker's oven with knobs and dials outside.

This crematorium chap told me that a fragile old lady took about 20 minutes and a 6 ft fellow up to an hour. You can look through a spy hole into the furnace while it is going full blast. At first all one can see is the end of the coffin, then the sides sort of blow out and the top caves in. After that there is just a pile of something burning steadily. At this stage the gas and air would be turned off, the door opened and a rake shoved inside to break things up a bit, before continuing with the incineration process.

At the end, after a cooling off period, what remains is pushed along a little passage at the back. The next stage is to run an electro-magnet over these rough remains so as to extract coffin nails and other interesting pieces of metal like stainless steel hip joints, knee caps and, what was popular at one time, pieces of shrapnel left in peoples bodies following the war.

After the denailing process as it is called, comes the final part of reducing the remains to fine ash. This is done on a grinding machine which looks very much like an old fashioned gramophone with the horn sticking up at the top. The remains are tipped into it, then pass through the grinders which are quite powerful as they often have to deal with bits of leg bone, pelvis and the odd skull.

After seeing the entire process of reducing a body to fine ash, I thought the whole thing a bit pathetic and, when my time comes, I would prefer to be buried outside where it is wet and windy. All this might sound morbid but what I am trying to say is that steeplejacking takes one into some strange places. I mentioned wet and windy because then you have to come down from the church steeple being mended and hang around waiting for the weather to improve. Therefore you get a lot of time to think.

For example when I am alone in a churchyard, waiting for the rain clouds to blow by, I tend to read the grave stones. Some are very interesting and there is one that particularly sticks in my mind. It is the grave stone of Joseph Spragg killed during a colliery disaster in 1873. He was buried in the pit, eventually brought out and buried again in a proper cemetery. Somehow I think Joseph would have liked that.

There was another gravestone where the deceased left strict instructions for all his sins to be listed—wine, women and dirty songs, the lot. I found that really funny and laughed for days after seeing it.

Looking down on Lancashire graveyards, I would say most are in poor condition with long grass and willow herb growing all over them. There is little or no attention paid to them. So I like the idea where the best tombstones are put up around the outer perimeter and the rest of the place covered in good green turf.

Other odd jobs I have to do from time to time include cleaning pigeon droppings from the tops of belfries and mending clocks stuck way up on the tops of towers. Often I have to do both jobs at the same time, also put up wire netting to prevent the pigeons returning to that particular toilet.

Now a funny thing happened on one of these jobs and it were a bit of a coincidence as well. Me father often used to help me after he had retired and we were high up in a church tower fixing some wire netting. Well it was about 11.30 one morning and we were banging away when I heard shuffling up the spiral stone staircase to the tower. The vicar then appeared and said,

"Would you stop hammering at about 11.45 as I have a funeral then."

Of course we agreed and I asked whose funeral it was. When we were told my father sat down all thoughtful. You see it were the man he had worked for, for over 40 years. So we watched with interest when the cortege arrived for the big man's funeral with a lot of black limousines and men in tall hats.

Me dad remained thoughtful but I took no more notice because funerals

Fred stops for a breather, and a few puffs, having fixed a new weather vane on Bury Parish Church.

had become everyday occasions to me. As I could not continue putting up the wire netting, I turned my attention to the church clock, which I also had to mend.

It had been beautifully made by a man called Bailey in Manchester and run well for years, until something went wrong with the chiming mechanism. I soon saw what was the matter. The weight, which drove the mechanism, had come off its pulley wheel and was resting on the spindle. So I said to my dad—to rouse him from his morbid thoughts like,

"If we can get that baulk of wood out of the corner, it could go across the top of the box to help lever up that weight."

Here I should explain that all the weights were suspended down an 80 ft long wooden shaft, from where we were to the bottom of the tower. The weight in question, that were giving the trouble, was about level with the top of this shaft, so it could be levered like I suggested.

Anyway we got the baulk of timber and put one end under the weight. My plan of campaign was to balance the timber across the top of the shaft ledge. Then when me dad held the weight upwards, I would simply slip the wire from the spindle back on to its proper pulley. Meanwhile they were just getting the coffin out of the hearse in front of the church.

"It's no good," said my father after straining away. "The ledge of the shaft is not high enough for the necessary leverage."

"Yes," I agreed. "It needs another 3 or 4 inches—like that half brick there."

So I picked up the brick, put it on top of the ledge and me dad again set about levering up the weight. This time he did it and I was able to replace the wire on its pulley. But we forgot about the half brick. As the baulk of wood was being removed, the brick fell off the ledge and went straight down that 80 ft wooden shaft.

By then the coffin was entering the church and things were becoming solemn among the congregation. No one but the vicar knew we were around and everyone else were concentrating on other matters. Well you can imagine that 80 ft of wooden shafting makes quite a good sounding box, amplifies everything no end.

There was this almighty crash which stopped those moving in their tracks—coffin bearers, organist, the lot—halfway up the aisle. I could see them all sort of frozen there and was a bit shaken like myself.

Not so me dad. A slow smile spread over his face which were stuck close to mine.

"What are you thinking?" I whispered and he whispered back,

"They must think he's woken up."

Apart from a passing interest in funerals, weddings and similar services, steeplejacks waiting in churches have other priorities. The main one as I have mentioned is the weather. It can be very frustrating whenever there is rain and it does a bit around Lancashire. If for example you are pointing some coping stones up a steeple, what people call a nice drop of afternoon rain can ruin a whole morning's work.

A steeplejack 200 ft up in the air also sees the weather a long way off. He can watch it over the next town—arriving there, giving them a downpour then leaving their roof tops all bright and shining in the sunshine while it comes your way. There is a sort of inevitability about it which requires patience.

I remember on one occasion how I spent hours pointing some 30 ft of coping stones at an incredibly difficult part of a church tower. Then the rain came and within seconds washed out every bit of mortar. You would never think I had ever done the job.

So what happens next is that I have to do the same job all over again. That means going down to the graveyard tap where ordinary people get water for flowers and steeplejacks more water for more cement. On this occasion I did

A steeplejack's eye view, from Bolton Parish church, November 1963.

it all again and it rained again and I did it a third time in one day.

In physical terms it means going up and down ladders with the thin handles of heavy buckets digging into your muscles. Recently after one of my television appearances I received a letter saying how lucky I was to live such a tranquil life high above the cares and troubles of this world.

I was tempted to reply "You must be joking", but there was a grain of truth in the letter. Yes I like my job and I do have close ups of the wonderful work built by my ancestors. It is an incredible one if you think about it.

Fred holds one of the stone pillars he made for Bolton Town Hall. Seen here high up on the scaffolding.

Bolton Town Hall showing the superb craftsmanship and care that went into designing and constructing such buildings in the past.

Within a short span of time, they put up those six-story mill houses, those 250 ft chimneys, those huge churches and town halls, laid railway lines, dug canals and mined coal, not to forget building those endless rows of terrace houses with pubs and corner shops.

You cannot help noticing them when you are all alone above this incredible world stretching to the circular horizon. Just as you cannot help admiring the work that went into a single chimney stack or church steeple. I have seen them from close-up and they are fantastic. Great big stones perched 200 ft up in the sky covered in incredible carvings. And all fitting perfectly, in an attempt to try to keep them up there forever.

That is why I try. I do not get much pleasure demolishing a chimney because I think of those fellows manhandling tens of thousands of bricks and tons of mortar to build the thing in the first place. It is the same with the churches and other buildings. They were not built by one or two keen religious types, but must have required a swarm of your ordinary working men.

Then you come to the other side of the coin. You can catch a glimpse of it in those old sepia photographs of the bosses and their work forces. In those days the bosses had good suits, wore hats and carried gold watches. Next look at the men with their sunken eyes in white faces, in thin vests and ill-fitting trousers over their skinny frames. They were literally worked to death in those mills and factories, also hacking out seams of coal for 10, 12 or 14 hours a day in spaces less than 2 ft high.

So those Victorian bosses, all living in beautiful mansions would erect churches to salve their consciences like. They were not all bad, but they benefitted from other peoples misery. No proper wages, no unions, no pensions, that was their creed. You just did as you were told and, like I said, worked yourself to death. Fortunately a few, like me dad, got through his 40 years in the filth of the bleach works despite the rats having a go at his dinner each working day.

There was another old friend of mine who came from a family of steeplejacks and had been one himself for decades. I remember him when I was a little lad, coughing and choking from the work he did on factory chimneys. There were no safety conditions then or a Welfare State either but he managed to survive and put a bit by for his old age.

"I got through, Fred," he once told me, "and now I am going to enjoy taking things easy." The next day he was knocked over and killed by a lettuce wagon going to market. It makes you think. You cannot help having odd thoughts doing the odd jobs we do.

The felling of the chimney at a water works pumping station. Note men protected by hard hats...

Chapter 6

Chimney Pieces

It was my friend Ken the Halle violinist who introduced me to his Uncle John. Ken was an enthusiastic amateur so far as chimneys were concerned, but he could not give them his full attention on account of the Brahms and Beethoven stuff. John on the other hand was very versatile. He seemed to have done everything in life including playing rugby, mining coal and sawing stone blocks. Just the chap, I decided to be my assistant.

Our first job together entailed demolishing a chimney for a firm at Croston, which is a little village on the way to Southport. Funnily enough the factory made chimney pots. That was interesting while the awkward bit concerned the chimney we had to fell. It were in a tight position between the works and a river. The local water authority had only just cleaned out that river and they told me, in no uncertain terms, not to drop a single brick in it.

Anyway John and I went through a routine which I shall cover in the next chapter. We cut away some of the base, put in wooden props and laid a fire round them. Then we went round and weakened the other side of the base. tension mounted in Croston when we lit the fire and the props were burned away. However the chimney went over just right and everything after that were a bit of an anti-climax.

Next came a monstrous chimney at a big spinning and weaving company. It was 200 ft high, octagonal in shape with a square base and had beautiful moulding round everything. It was also 6 ft thick. Hammering holes through 6 ft of perfectly laid Victorian brickwork can be painful. John and I had to stick at it because once you have accepted a job it is yours.

The job after that was unbelievable—another 200 footer which had to fall along a 60 ft wide slot. There was no way of avoiding it. A street lay on one side and a mill wall on the other. The owners and their insurers were not the only ones shaking in their shoes, I can tell you. John and I again did all the hand cutting work but very, very carefully this time.

The mill chimney was due to come down on a Sunday morning when there would be less traffic to divert. That Saturday night, we checked everything before leaving work. The cuts had been made, the props were in position and the fire laid. That stack was ready and waiting to come down inside, I hoped, the slot.

Our television was on when I arrived home and, while talking to Alison in the kitchen, I heard the newsman saying,

"Here's a chimney that went wrong."

I raced into the front room just in time to see a chimney come crashing down on a factory building. When the newsman said the place was in Yorkshire, the relief was terrific. It was not however a relief for the Yorkshire firm. After being cut in two, that factory is still shut and people out of work. So you see we chimney fellers have our responsibilities.

Sunday morning came with the police and the usual sightseers gathered around waiting for Fred Dibnah to succeed or fail. I took a last look at the yard, down which the stack must fall, with the side of the factory beside it.

"Lancashire has got to do better than Yorkshire." I remarked to John as the fire was being lit. The flames rose, the props burned away and the stack fell in a dead straight line along the yard. A couple of factory windows were broken by bouncing bricks but they let me off that.

Nothing succeeds like success and pride comes before a fall, so they say. Not long afterwards a council gave me an official order to dismantle a couple of chimneys. The first was within 19 ft of a main railway line, so the order stipulated that this stack must be taken down brick by brick. Well, after my precision job at the mill, I had become a bit swell-headed like. I went to see the first of the two chimneys and noted it leaned away from the railway.

"We can do this one the easy way," I said to John and he agreed. After all the other way would mean hammers and chisels for weeks.

I chose a bank holiday Saturday to have a go at that chimney. There were not a lot of people about when we cut the fire hole, put in the props and set fire to them. The props burned away, the fire went out but still the wretched chimney stood beside the railway line. By then darkness was on us and we had to leave it for the night.

That night I rang Ken the violinist, his father and one or two other fellows I knew about making an early morning start. We were on site at 6 am and by 8.30 the chimney was down without a piece anywhere near the railway. It seemed a perfect job.

But someone must have seen and reported us for I received a sharp letter from the council concerned.

"Dear Mr Dibnah," it began unpromisingly, "You have violated the contract, also put us in a most critical position with the railway..."

After that came chapter and verse ending with 'since you have broken the contract, it is now null and void'. Between this bad beginning and even worse end, they mentioned I could not expect to be paid for the first chimney or even allowed near the second, despite it being situated in open country.

Now I knew one or two influential people and sought their advice on the matter. What each separately told me amounted to the same thing,

"Creep " said one, "like mad."

"Write a letter in your best copper plate," the other said, "to the Borough Engineer asking for an interview."

It was a formal interview. The chap who doled out demolition work for the council was there determined to shoot me down in flames. Yet he was in the right. I had been contracted to take the chimney beside the railway down brick by brick. Instead I had felled it with an attempt at secrecy. Therefore I had broken the contract as they said. End of argument.

More often than not however the best form of defence is to go off at an angle. I pointed out that many of the other chimneys felled in town by the explosive boys had gone wrong. My method, I pressed on, might seem old fashioned but the success rate proved its worth.

"I tell you what," I said. 'I'll bring down your second chimney free of charge if you will pay me for the first one which is, after all, safely down."

Brickwork is drilled out from the base of a chimney.

Felling of John Bright's chimney, Woodbine Street, Rochdale.

"Well..." the Borough Engineer nibbled at this bait, so I continued.

"And you can light the fire yourself."

He fancied the idea and we agreed on a certain Thursday. By then there was a Force 10 gale blowing. Normally I would have put the firing off and left the chimney 'on the sticks' as we say, but the big man from the town hall was still coming with all his entourage. Moreover the local newspaper happened to have been alerted and would be present to record the event.

So the Borough Engineer duly lit the fire and the newspaper photographers took pictures of him doing it. After that no one seemed to realise what was going wrong, except John and me.

Besides burning the props, that high wind set fire to nearby grass and bushes. This caused the men from the council together with the press men to retreat some 200 yards. It left John and I gazing unbelievably up at the chimney. The props had long gone from the one side and the other had been weakened to ensure a fall, yet the stack stayed where it was. Or rather it swayed some 3 ft this way then the other like a willow wand.

It was crazy, it was dangerous but we had to do something. Hauling our 50 ton hydraulic jack out of the truck, we applied pressure. Fortunately we succeeded and the chimney came down to a ragged cheer from the distant spectators.

When I went to talk to them, it were all about fine balancing and counteracting high wind forces. As I said afterwards to John,

"It had to look as if we knew what we were doing."

This brought me another job beside a railway line, which I would have preferred to avoid. Railway people are very alert and suspicious of anything going on anywhere near their bit of track. In this case it were only a shunting yard and I thought we would have no trouble.

But once more it was one of my minor disasters. There was not much about to harm and one of my fellows had acquired some extra fuel in the form of big rubber buffers. We packed these among the timber and lit the touchpaper which covered the whole shunting yard in dense black smoke. Not only that, the heat was not enough to bring down the chimney.

We had to put out the fire and start again. It sounded simple enough until I discovered there was no water anywhere near the site. I searched frantically around and what I did find was a fleet of bulldozers each of which could take 45 gallons of water at a time. This they did, then tipped it over the flames beneath the chimney. It were a shambles.

As soon as the flames were out, my men chiselled away another six inches of brickwork, lit another fire—this time without rubber buffers—and the

A spectacular end for the Ocean Mill chimney, Bolton.

thing came crashing down. It nearly landed on a very posh limousine which had come our way. Out stepped an equally posh character who said in a pained voice,

"Do you people realise that you are interfering with the running of my railway."

This put some of the fellows backs up and one said,

"It ain't your bloody railway. It's supposed to belong to the nation."

"Oh well," said the character before getting back into his limousine, "you've done a good job, but don't interfere with my railway again."

*Over she goes!
The chimney at
Pickups Clay Pipe
Works, Horwich is
brought safely down.*

Dereliction at Alder Mill, Leigh, with the chimney ready to be felled.

Fred's stalwart assistant, Donald, holds on to the life-supporting rope at the foot of a chimney.

After that the chimney jobs I had to tackle got progressively harder. It may not seem possible, after all a chimney is a chimney, but there can be complications.

The next job called for John and I to re-point a 200 ft stack from top to bottom. This was a task which required erecting a lot of scaffolding then getting down to solid uninterrupted work. At the time unfortunately John was having personal problems and had to leave me. He did so after most of the repointing was done, but it left me with scaffolding still up the chimney and no assistant to get it down.

So who better to call in than Alison. She left her unimportant house work and spent the next few days moving tackle.

"You'll have to find another permanent assistant," she said at one stage and I said,

"Yes, there is someone I have in mind."

The someone was Donald who I have already mentioned in connection with the dangerous well which nearly killed me. His grandparents and parents once owned a big building company on the outskirts of town, but what happened to the family business was most unfortunate.

The powers that be were building a motorway and compulsory purchased the entire premises. Donald was left with a house to live in and a bob or two at the bank but no business. He used to walk his dog past my place and we got into conversation.

"If you ever need a hand..." he had once said, so I decided to take him up on it.

Our first job together was a council one. I should not say this—for all work is bread-and-butter—but town hall people can make a hard life harder. And, when you get two lots of town hall people in on an act, it can become very tricky indeed. In the end you can spend more time and trouble than the job is worth.

In this particular case, two councils had gone about building a rubbish incinerator plant with a 200 ft chimney. I do not mean using an old chimney, of which there were plenty about, but making a new one with all the resources of 20th century technology.

Well that incineration plant was commissioned with a fanfare of trumpets. It were the greatest thing since sliced bread. True there were some teething troubles, but we can forget about that. Rubbish was being burned in the new technology chimney and within 18 months the stack was cracked right the way up on both sides.

Then the in-fighting began. The project had been started by one council then transferred to the other. So, when it went wrong, it was somebody else's responsibility. Many of these councillors went to a pub I knew and one day as they were skirting round the subject, I asked,

"When are you going to do something about that useless chimney?"

They hummed and hawed about whether it was useless but, before the time the thing reached 2 years old, smoke was coming out about 60 ft from the top and even simple folk were saying,

"What have they done now like?"

Anyway one day my phone rang. The call came from an engineer in the rubbish incineration plant. Could I come and have a look at the chimney? I went round and we talked about it for sometime. In the end I said my ladders would have to go up in order for me to take a closer look at the crack and see how bad it was.

So I laddered their chimney and on a Sunday morning, when the fire was out, went up to carry out my inspection. The crack was so bad you could put a packet of cigarettes in it—sideways. To prove it, I carried a camera with me and ran off three rolls of film. When these pictures were developed, everyone got all excited about them and agreed that the nearly new chimney would have to come down.

The bit about that job that I remember and which always amused me, was some consultants I had to consult. The council asked me to send my 108 prints to a real double barrelled architectural firm down in Middlesex, named 'Somebody, Somebody & Somebody'.

"Dear Mr Dibnah', they wrote back, "please send us seven sets of all your photographs.''

"I have no idea what they did with those 756 pictures, but you have to humour such people.

The trouble is you have to humour more and more people these days. It is no longer a simple matter doing what should be done. There are layers of people to get through—factory owners, property developers, council men and their consultants. The mill owners never have any money and the developers are after quick money. The council people are experts in covering themselves, while the consultants have it made.

To make matters more complicated, most demolition jobs are put out to firms that specialise in them. I do the chimney side for a very good demolition company, but there are some real cowboys in that line of business. They tell you one thing and the authorities tell you another. Apart from risking your own life, dropping a chimney can do thousands of pounds worth of damage. Apart from hitting buildings or falling across railway lines, there may be sewers or subterranean workings which would not take kindly to a 1,000 tons of bricks descending on them.

One cowboy outfit I remember had Donald and I start and stop three times on a job they had never wrapped up properly with the council. The head of the outfit, who wore a bobble hat, dark glasses and drove an Alpha Romeo would keep telling me,

"Not to worry Fred. I'll sort the bother out. Be on to you later this evening.''

Then a fortnight would go by before he rang again to say.

"You can start tomorrow Fred.''

"As it happens I'm tied up tomorrow.''

"But this one is red hot urgent Fred. I've ironed out all the problems.''

When someone tells me that I do begin to get worried. Once again we dropped everything and turned up on his site. Once more nothing went according to plan. Again the king of the cowboys said he would sort out the council people.

So another week or two went by before he asked me to attend a site meeting. When Donald and I got there, it was to see two Irish lads hammering away at the bottom of the chimney.

"Come on Donald,'' I said, "we've had enough of this.''

Fortunately we pulled out of that particular exercise. The chimney finally fell over in the dark, ripping about 20 yards off a factory wall while the flying bits and pieces broke windows across the other side of the road.

I am not trying to be clever and big-headed about all this. Few people

Fred checks the pit props under the chimney at Pickups Clay Pipe Works before the fire is laid.

Fred lights the fire.

realise the problems involved in chimney work, also the forces released when a stack comes down. There was one horror right in the middle of Bolton which illustrates my two points of problems and forces.

This chimney, that few people ever noticed or thought about, was situated beside a mill and right next door to the market place. It had been built around 1860 to a height of 220 ft. The brick thickness at the top was 9 inches and on top of that the builders placed a huge stone head. This capping weighed about 20 tons and had a 3 ft overhang. They created what you might call a hundred-year time bomb.

To be fair to the old builders, for the Victorians built well, their chimney should have been regularly maintained. All the sulphurous and acidic smoke that goes up chimneys can be kept in hand by regular maintenance—like inspections, new linings and general renovations. But Lancashire mill owners were notorious for not wanting to part with the green stuff.

"It'll do until next year." they would say, when their engineers dared to bring up the matter.

So year after year, then decade after decade ticked by with smoke gnawing away the insides of that chimney.

There comes a time when something has to be done. In the case of the particularly nasty chimney I had to put right, I would imagine the engineer had been told not to spend much on it, which meant a patch job. So round the brick stack he wrapped what you might call an iron corset then he attached that to the factory wall by steel wires. I would lay a bet he was not even thanked for doing a cheap job.

Meanwhile the history of the country went on. There were business booms and depressions, wars and outbreaks of peace. People were born, lived and died. All the time, the chimney remained up there—unnoticed, taken for granted, with the fumes passing through it and eating away more and more of the brickwork. Then one day, which unfortunately happened to me in my lifetime, a piece fell off into the mill yard as a kind of warning shot. At long last, it was necessary to take positive action.

"Fred's the chap," everyone said, "for this one."

On reaching the top of the chimney and looking inside, I saw there was literally nothing left of the brickwork. I had suspected this when drilling holes for my ladder because the drill kept going straight through. The only thing which held up that 220 ft stack, with its 20 ton capping on less than 9 ins of brick, were the iron corsets. By this stage people were saying,

"We are leaving this entirely to you, Fred. It's your problem."

I knew the way to do it, which is not the same as saying it was going to be

The end of John Bright's chimney—Fred stands on the fallen remains, a job well done.

simple. I would have to start my scaffolding some way down the stack then build a series of platforms, with as many bracing pieces as possible, up to a stout support under the overhang. Then would come what you might call the moment of truth.

As a matter of morbid interest, three-quarters of the deaths among steeplejacks occur because of what can happen next. They would build their last staging support under the capping stones, then cut through angle ironwork to get at the stones themselves. At that stage the bloody lot would fall smashing the staging and killing the men.

I managed to avoid this on that horror chimney by building substantial supports from strong pipes and stout pieces of timber. However what nagged away at me all the time was the fact that the structure base on which my scaffolding and staging had been mounted were rotten. There was an ominous quiver when I cut the iron ring under the stone overhang but—as I lived to tell of it—everything held. After that Donald and I were able to get the capping stones down one by one, then gently dismantled the rest of the horror.

However a funny thing happened during the otherwise precarious exercise. Whenever I am on particularly difficult jobs, there are important looking people superintending like. They generally drive Mercedes cars and carry real leather brief cases with brass corners on them. One such character always seemed to be around when Donald and I were putting up ladders. As I have said that were not easy in case, due to the rotten brickwork, so we were very cautious hooking on each ladder in turn.

At the end of it all this character came up to me and said,

"I have always been intrigued as to how ladders went up chimneys."

"How did you think they went up then?" I asked.

"Well," he said, "I imagined they were put end to end and connected, before being reared up the chimney."

Donald, who was standing nearby, could not help laughing but I managed to keep a straight face.

"It would be a bit difficult," I pointed out, "holding your foot on the bottom rung while trying to heave the other 199 feet upwards."

"I suppose it would be," said the chap, which made me wonder how he came to own a Mercedes.

Chapter 7

Trade Secrets

Now the time has come to reveal a few trade secrets though not many will profit from them. Whenever people start chatting to me, sooner or later the conversation comes round to the inevitable question. I have been asked the same question a million times and here it is,

"How do you get up there?"

Some people believe chimneys have ladders already hooked in place. The short answer to that one is they have not. Holes have to be drilled, hooks knocked in and the ladders fitted one by one up a near vertical brick surface to a height of 2-300 feet. Then, at the very top, there may be a capping stone projecting 2-3 feet outwards. It seems impossible yet here are the tricks of my trade, also the tools and methods used.

Remembering my art school days, I have done Drawings 1, 2 and 3 as reproduced in this book. Fig. No.1 of my first drawing shows a strange looking instrument called a dog or quite often a hook because of the hook on top. It is made of iron, is about 9 inches long and resembles one of those things people knock in their garden wall for attaching a clothes line. A steeplejack's dog is much bigger and much, much stronger, the iron bar from which it is made being three-quarters of an inch in diameter.

Turning to Fig. No.2, this is the type of chisel for making holes in the joints of chimney brick work. It is a special sort of chisel which cannot be bought in shops. There are two ways of obtaining such an instrument. The first is find a blacksmith and the second to make it yourself.

When I began steeplejacking, I soon realised the need for lots of dogs, chisels, various brackets and other iron implements which could only be made by a blacksmith or someone with a forge. I bought from smiths to start with, then decided to have my own forge. I also had to improvise. A 56 lb weight served as an anvil until the travelling grave digger, who I mentioned previously, helped me unearth one. As for the furnace, I used a pile of old thrown-out fire bricks and the draught was supplied by me mum's Hoover. From then onwards, I made all my own iron work and have since graduated to a proper forge.

Referring now to Fig. No.3 the piece of wood shown is called a skid. It is a packing piece tied, as I have shown, to the back of the ladder to hold that away from the chimney wall. The reason for fitting skids is they allow room for your feet to rest naturally on the rungs of the ladder and not be forced outwards. This is rather important when climbing high chimneys.

Some steeplejacks prefer to have iron skids fitted to the backs of their ladders but I stick to old fashioned way for the following reason. If I come across some unforeseen protrusion, like a bit of collar towards the top of the chimney, then a fixed iron skid becomes a drawback to remove. With a tied-on wooden skid, the strings are released and it can be moved up or down a couple of rungs.

The drawing shows both the basic construction of a wooden skid and how it is attached to the ladder. The skid is simply a length of 1 inch timber screwed to two 9 inch blocks. If both pieces of string, holding the skid to the back of the ladder, pass inside the blocks, then no sideways slippage can take place.

Fig. No.4 illustrates how the ladders are lashed to a dog. A length of rope about 6 ft long is used having a loop spliced on one end and a bit of whipping round the tail. The loop goes over the hook of the dog, round one side of the ladder, back over the hook and the other side of the ladder. It again goes over the hook before being attached to a rung by a clove hitch. With this method, the ladder can be lifted slightly away from the wall, also move up and down, yet is well secured to the dog.

The same illustration depicts how the ladders fit together. There are other ways of doing this, but I prefer the arrangement shown because it is simple, strong and fool proof. You can put ladders on the ground without damaging or clogging the brackets. There is nothing worse than being up a chimney in howling gale trying to dig dirt out of fance ladders.

Fig. No.5 shows the type of hole into which a dog is fitted. When the bricks are in a reasonable condition the dog need only be driven about 2½ inchs. The real trick here is having the little bit of wood shown in black. Steeplejacks fitting dogs carry a pocketful of these plugs which they thump into the holes they have chiselled between the bricks. I make my plugs about an inch long, which is sufficient to hold the dog and will come out easily afterwards instead of being left in to rot. I also point every hole before leaving a chimney so the surface is ready and waiting for the next time someone has to scale it.

Now comes the bit which the chap with the Mercedes I mentioned and most other people do not realise or understand. How to get up there. How to fit ladders up a 2-300ft near-vertical chimney without killing yourself or anyone else. Each steeplejack ladder is 16 ft long, has 21 rungs at 9 inch centres and every fifth rung is made of iron. These iron rungs are very handy for hanging a bosun's chair as I shall describe later. You can attach the chair

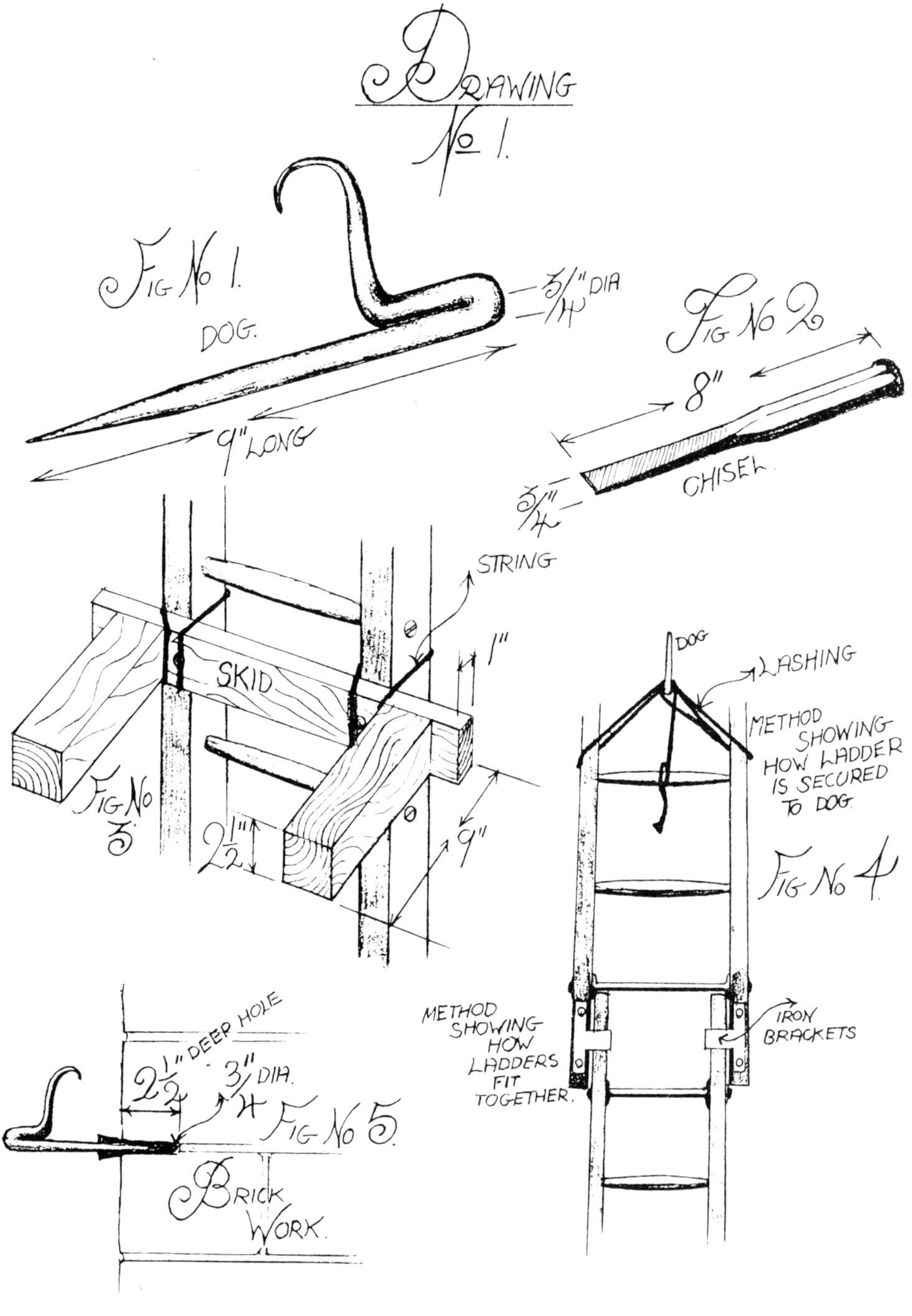
Drawing No 1.
Fig No 1.
DOG.
3/4" DIA
9" LONG
Fig No 2
8"
CHISEL
3/4"
STRING
1"
SKID
Fig No 3.
2 1/2"
9"
DOG
LASHING
METHOD SHOWING HOW LADDER IS SECURED TO DOG.
Fig No 4.
METHOD SHOWING HOW LADDERS FIT TOGETHER.
IRON BRACKETS
1" DEEP HOLE
2 1/2
3/4" DIA.
Fig No 5.
BRICK WORK.

pulley to any of these and dangle with confidence.

The first move, which is done on the ground, is to tie skids on the ladders as I have already described. The next is to attach lashings—the ones by which ladders will be secured to dogs—loosely round the bottom rungs of each ladder. These lashings are initially used to carry spare dogs aloft as I have sketched on the second ladder at the bottom of Drawing No.2.

Here is a great trick which an old steeplejack taught me.

"During the winter," he said, "you should warm the dogs on the nearest boiler. It makes all the differenece to working with cold lumps of iron."

So when I am taking 2½ hours to ladder a 250 ft chimney in wintertime, I have my assistant sending me up these beautiful hot pieces of iron to use, which is like having a built-in central heating system.

Starting with Fig. No.1 of Drawing No.2, the first ladder is propped against the chimney with its skid facing outwards, just as a householder does to clean the guttering. The steeplejack then fits a dog about three or four feet from the ground and another three quarters way up the leaning ladder. These two dogs should be dead in line and have loose lashings hung ready from them as shown.

The ladder is then turned over and pushed in against a loose skid or a couple of bricks lying on the ground. It is then in the positions of Fig. No.2 when the lower lashing is wrapped round and tied with a clove hitch as I have previously described. It is perfectly safe to start climbing the lower half of the first ladder held in such a way so as to catch hold of the next loose lashing. This is also wrapped round and tied, thereby securing the first ladder to the chimney.

From then onwards, an experienced steeplejack keeps going upwards. It means he must have everything he needs with him—hammer, chisel, a pocketful of plugs, spare lashings and the next dog to be fitted stuck in his belt. He will also take with him a pulley wheel with a rope through it. His assistant remains on the ground to feed the succession of ladders and other gear up to him, like further lashings and boiler-warmed dogs.

On reaching the top of the first ladder, the steeplejack puts one of his legs down the back of the ladder while the other remains on the outside. This leaves him with both hands free to reach up and drill the next hole for the dog in his belt. I am a bit short myself, so I can only reach about 4 ft above the top of a ladder, but it does not matter. What really matters is to fit each iron dog securely in the chimney brickwork. It is a sort of life or death necessity.

Once the dog is in place, the pulley wheel is hung from its hook with the

Drawing No 26

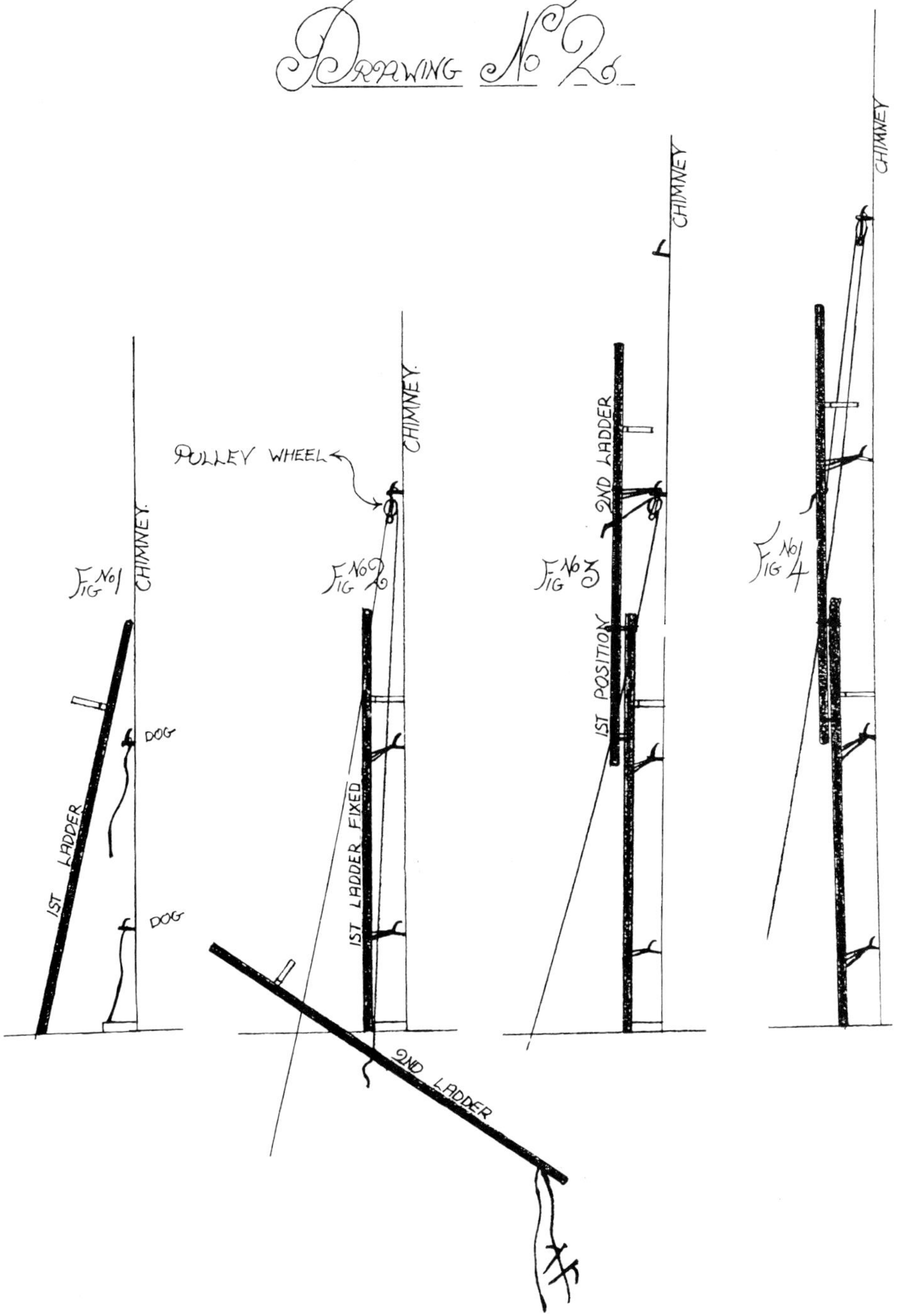

other end of the rope down to where the second ladder is lying. This next ladder is tied nine rungs from its top. The assistant then pulls it up while I move down from my position at the top of the first ladder to about the half way mark.

When the second ladder arrives, it cannot go any higher than the position shown in Fig. No.3 because the knot on the ladder is almost level with me pulley wheel. So, because of my taking up a lower position, I am able to use the two new lashings and dogs made available to me. These lashings help tie the second ladder as shown in a temporary position.

I then proceed to climb the rest of the way up the second ladder, hook one leg over to steady myself as before and fit the dog shown at the top of Fig. No.3. To understand what happens next, refer to Drawing No.2, Fig. No.4. It will be seen that the pulley wheel is removed from the lower dog and taken to the upper one. During this operation the rope of the pulley remains tied to the second ladder and held by the man on the ground.

Red ladders to the sky—note the way the ladder (right) is attached to the chimney by means of rope lashed to a dog.

While he is doing that, I descend again to undo the two temporary lashings leaving one on the ladder and one on the dog as shown in Fig. No.5. Then my assistant pulls the second ladder further up. It is illustrated hanging in the air and looks dangerous, yet all is safe as I am on the fixed ladder below it. Once you have done the job a few times, these moves become automatic.

The next important part is to fit the ends of the two ladders together in their proper sockets—see Fig. No.6. From there it is easy to catch hold of the lashing hanging from the dog and tie the lower half of the second ladder to it. As this ladder is now being held in two places, also by the pulley rope, it is safe to proceed further up and put another lashing on the dog holding the pulley.

Once again, exactly as before, the steeplejack steadies himself on top of the second ladder to drill yet another hole for the next dog. Once again he shifts the pulley wheel to it and the third ladder is hauled up from below with more lashings and dogs attached. Fig. 7. In this way two men can fit six or seven ladders to a chimney within an hour. Once I have explained how the ladders get up there people then ask,

"What happens when you reach that bit at the top, where it sticks out two or three feet?"

Well, thank the Lord, there are not many of them left. Those huge capping stones, with which the Victorians liked to finish off their chimneys, have nearly all been taken down as I described in the previous chapter. However my last drawing shows how the overhang problem is overcome.

On arriving under the overhang, it is essential that the top of the highest vertical ladder is well and truly secured to the chimney. If there is any ironwork about, and there generally is, extra lashings are made round them. Then with the pulley wheel hooked on to the top iron rung of the highest vertical ladder, the loose end of the rope is used to bring up the last ladder of all.

This last ladder to come up must have half a dozen good lashings tied to it, because the assistant on the ground will know what is involved. The middle of the ladder reaches about level with the pulley and is tied, leaving a bit of slack as shown. That allows the ladder to be tilted back so its upper end passes outside the chimney cap while the lower end bears against the vertical ladder. Of course it is a bit more difficult than that at 200 ft. You have to wrap your legs round the rungs and whoever is below has to keep pulling like hell.

People always think climbing under the overhang must be awful, but there is not much difference to the usual way. It is still a ladder and your feet will not slide off the rungs. Anyone can prove this by leaning a ladder against the side of a house and having a go on the first few rungs. Even so, the main point at the top of a chimney is to make sure the overhang ladder is properly fastened. (Fig. 8)

This is done by lashing the bottom rung of the leaning-outwards ladder to the corresponding rung of the upright one. You then move up a bit and do the same between the next dog and the upright ladder rung nearest to it. After that comes a third extra lashing to the top rung of the upright ladder before taking the bull by the horns, so to speak, to climb under and over the stone cap.

At this final stage, the steeplejack must have everything handy—hammer and chisel, the last dog in his belt and a couple of lashings round his neck. For when he gets over the capping stone, the dog has to be fitted and the loose, quivering end of the overhung ladder secured to it. This operation is the one which divides the men from the boys.

Bringing ladders down can be just as exciting. For the reverse operation, the steeplejack climbs to the top of the chimney with his hammer, a trowel and half a bucket of mortar. His first operation is to take the pulley wheel off the rope, which is then passed over the hook of the top most dog, then tied round the middle of the outward leaning ladder. The jack then undoes the top lashings and comes down the ladder with the bucket of mortar to undo the lower lashings.

The leaning ladder is now free to be eased out of position. It does not simply fall downwards because counteracting that is the weight of 200 ft of rope now running over a dog which is ¾ inch in diameter. In effect pulley wheels help in hauling ladders upwards while the dog acts as a brake when lowering them. After releasing lashings, the steeplejack knocks out each dog in turn with its wooden plug, then using the trowel and mortar, seals the hole.

Working on a 200 ft chimney, it takes about half an hour to do a good job of taking out the dogs and plugs, also pointing the holes. Some jacks are quicker, but they leave the plugs in the holes and throw everything down—dogs, lashings, the lot. The right way, when you begin to be loaded up with too many dogs and lashings, is to attach several to the next ladder being lowered down to the ground.

One problem remains even when you and all the ladders are back on the ground. Remember they have all been lowered by the rope running over the dog at the top of the chimney. The obvious solution is to pull one end of this

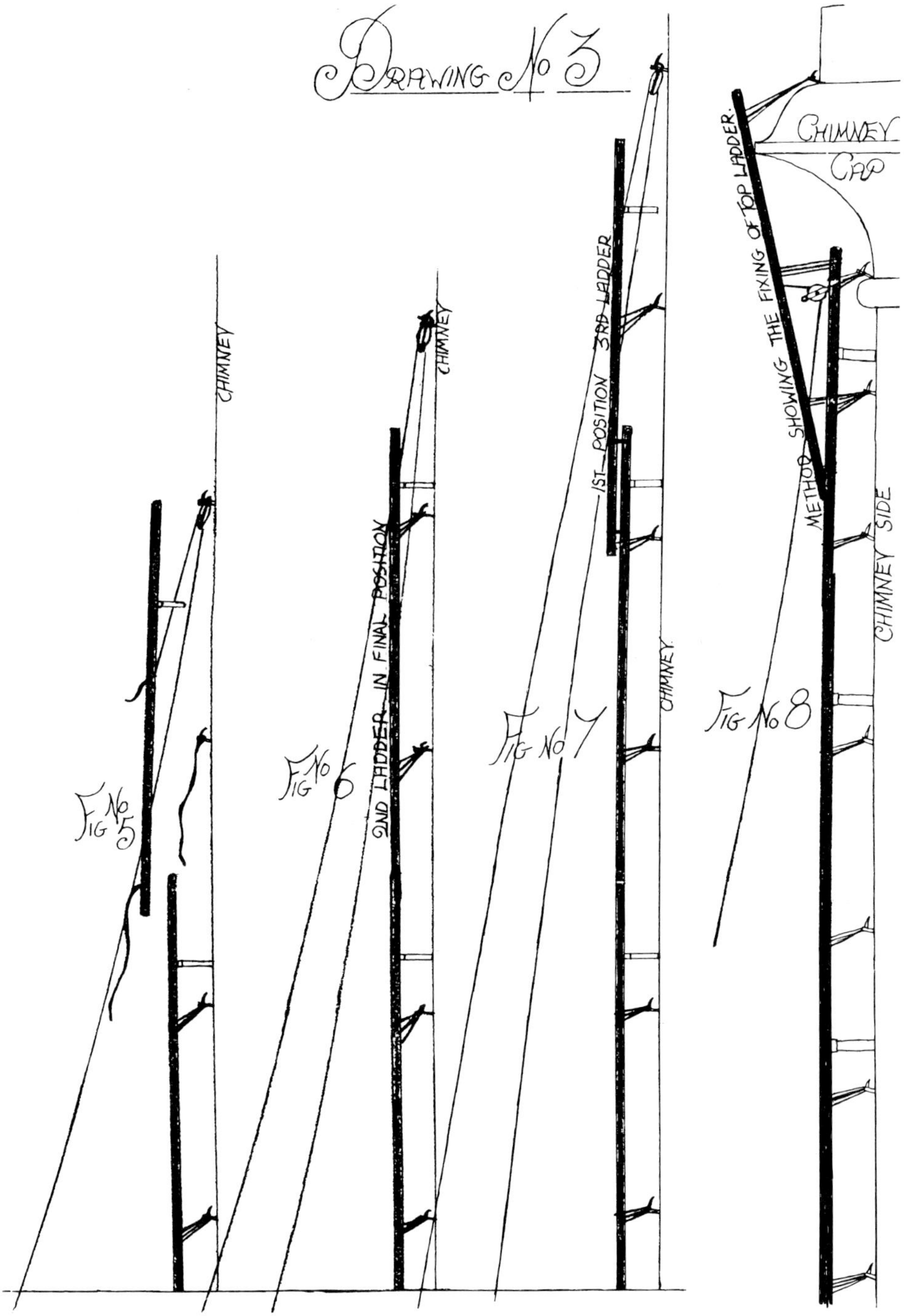
DRAWING No 3
CHIMNEY
FIG No 5
CHIMNEY
FIG No 6
2ND LADDER IN FINAL POSITION
FIG No 7
1ST POSITION 3RD LADDER
CHIMNEY.
FIG No 8
METHOD SHOWING THE FIXING OF TOP LADDER.
CHIMNEY CAP
CHIMNEY SIDE

rope down when the other or tail end of the rope should go up and over the dog. However it would not work that way. As one side grows lighter, due to the diminishing length, the rope begins to travel at increasing speed and will actually knot itself round the dog at the top. This would leave the steeplejack with his rope tied to the top of the chimney and everyone very amused.

The proper method to get everything off the dog is a bit of an Indian rope trick. This entails having both ends of the rope on the ground and tieing them together with a piece of string about 10 ft long. On pulling one side, up goes the string part. It can look as if the rope is rising on its own, hence the name Indian rope trick. Anyway up it goes and the idea is to get both ends of the string over the dog. You then give a sharp tug which breaks the string and the rope comes tumbling down.

There is another little trick which I could have mentioned before, only it would have complicated matters at the time. I take a piece of steel tubing about 3 inches long up the chimney to put over the top dog before fitting it. This short tube revolves on the dog with the moving rope instead of rubbing too hard on a bare dog. The tubing in effect acts like a small pulley. It also prevents ruining lengths of good rope which cost a great deal of money.

Laddering a chimney is only the first step to getting up there like. The next is to erect scaffolding and staging. To do that means fitting other pulleys

Fred at his most content, dangling in a bosun's chair, and cigarette in one hand!

for my bosun's chair and hauling up great baulks of timber.

A bosun's chair—if all the ropes and tackle are in order—gives a wonderful sense of security. You know the rope will hold a couple of tons and your weight is nowhere near that. Nevertheless it pays to look after equipment because if a rope breaks you are dead. Whenever I get on my bosun's chair, I give it a little bounce to see if it is safe or not. It has never broken yet, but at that stage I am all ready to leap on the ladder if it does.

Putting up scaffolding and staging is a long business, so I will not go into too many details. I begin with two hefty pieces of timber which are pinned on either side of the chimney circumferance working from my bosun's chair Then long steel rods go through holes already drilled in the end of each piece, before tightening the timbers with nuts on the threaded ends of the rods. It is a bit tricky but makes for a secure job.

People do not realise that the poles and planks which are put up round the tops of chimneys run to 22 ft in length. They therefore have to be handled with care and very firmly secured. A 100 miles an hour wind might blow during the night and the staging should be there next morning instead of scattered over half the neighbourhood.

Wind is every steeplejacks enemy. Planks for example must always be held edge-on to the wind and, even in a light breeze, they give you a floating sort of feeling. Turn them sideways and you are away.

Dibnah's flying buckets in action at British Hardware & Tools Ltd, 1968.

Fixing new iron bands to the chimney of J. & J. Heyes, Leigh.

Chimneys also sway despite the day being calm. There is a movement from side to side even on the best built chimneys with not a crack in it. The feeling is a peculiar one as if something is not quite right. The only way I can describe the sensation is to say it is like after drinking five or six pints. You feel safe, you know you are safe , but it is a bit odd.

Another problem with chimney work which interested me from when I were a lad was how to lower loads of bricks. Some jacks would get a skip from the mill, tie a rope to each corner then, with a series of ropes and pulleys, haul it to the top. There they would load the skip until the bottom started creaking. They would have the tail rope wrapped round a lamp post or something substantial and release this very carefully. It were all rather primitive.

One day I had an idea of using two milk churns, the empty one going up as the full one came down. I thought having a brake drum in the system should work better than four strong men. So I started at the age of 17 to invent something to do the trick.

I went to the local motor scrap metal yard and unearthed a rear wheel brake unit—not a hydraulic one, but the kind which works off an iron rod. I brought it back to my shed and played about with it for many a week. Outside was a pole about 30 ft high to represent the chimney with a 56 lb weight on one end and 27 lb on the other.

After a lot of trial and error, I rigged up my system on a real chimney. I hauled up the empty churn, filled it with bricks and let it travel half way down, easing then stopping the loaded churn with the brake.

'Great!' I thought. 'I've done the trick.'

But that was not a true test. A true test would be to take the brake right off and let the loaded churn travel at dropping speed until the empty churn had come up and was just underneath the staging. All I had achieved so far was to lower the loaded churn cautiously with a partial stop in the middle.

On the next load therefore, I let the brake right off. The loaded churn certainly went like a bomb and I watched the empty churn hurtling towards me. When I applied the brake, it seemed to slow things down, but I did not know what else was going wrong.

What went wrong was that the loaded churn decided to go off on its own. Mesmerised I watched it smash into the corner of a boiler house, flattening everything as if run over by a steam roller. So I went down to survey the damage which seems to plague the efforts of us inventors and original thinkers.

The real cause of the trouble was that the attachments holding the churn

more money for my steam engine hobby. I cannot remember what I said to the Rotarians but that speech helped me to get two sacks of rivets.

When I got my steam roller, I thought of calling it Thunderbolt for a joke like. You see it could only do 4 miles an hour as it weighed all of 13 tons. Then I thought of naming the thing Alison. I hoped to gain a bit of grace back by doing so. After all, there is not every woman who has a steam roller named after her.

Because of their speed, or lack of it, steam rollers take a long time getting anywhere. The funny part is we steam roller and tractor men find driving our monsters easier when we have had a few in us than when we are stone sober. Drink sort of eases the pain. For example it feels less bumpy under the iron wheels and the racket going on becomes subdued.

However the main trouble with taking a lovely old steam roller for a run is that the roads are full of motor cars doing diabolical things. They do not seem to realise that though I can stop or start my roller, just like their motor cars, it must be done in a careful kind of way.

This can become a bit tricky on approaching traffic lights. Such lights seem to attract car drivers when there is a steam roller ahead. They must be in front of the steam roller in order to get smartly away from the traffic lights. So they nip between the red light and my monster. What they do not seem to realise is that I am unable to see exactly where they are while I am trying to bring my steam roller to a stop. If they knew the peril they were in, such drivers would think twice.

Another source of trouble arises from the genuine interest people have in steam engines. As they whizz past me in their motor cars most drivers turn round. That means they are driving forwards but looking backwards. Once I was going up a long hill at the top of which a bus stood at a bustop. The driver of the car which overtook me was so interested in my steam roller, he drove right the way up that long hill, looking round all the time—until he ran into the back of the bus.

Steam engines may not have to call at petrol stations but they need plenty of coal and water. The authorities do a Nelson, turning a blind eye on my activities, but really it is illegal to take water from hydrants. You can apply for a licence through, in my opinion, they should pay me a fee for testing their water hydrants because half are out of order. At least I put them right befor leaving.

My particular engine will do 7 to 8 miles on 80 gallons of water. So I have to use what I can get. It generally ends up with me calling the wife and kids to rally round on this urgent family matter. Lucky they do because if the level went too low there would be an explosion waking up the unlucky neighbourhood I happened to be passing through at the time.

If you have a steam roller or traction engine, you will need a great caravan at the back, like a sort of support vehicle. Mine has beds under which I put the coal and cupboards for my oil cans. It also holds Alison, the kids, our dog and a little corner cupboard for jam butties. The dog quite likes my steam roller but he will sit on the board at the front—I presume to see where he is going. This means he can jump off at any time and, as we roll along he changes colour from white to dirty grey.

In the early years of our marriage, things looked a bit fraught between Alison and I where important matters like steam engines were concerned. To tell the truth, we were quite close to divorce proceedings. Fortunately, as our married life rolled on, my wife Alison became used to my other wife Alison the steam roller and even began to like her, I think.

Steam rollers do sometimes present problems...'Alison' gets bogged down on entering the new garden.

Mind you, men who fancy steam engines can be a bit peculiar. Very few of the ones I know are married. They seem to think that wives and steam engines just do not mix. Worse still, they tend to look down on any woman, wife or not, who tries to get into their steam engine circle.

"Women," they say, "cannot begin to appreciate a steam engine." Worst still, they try getting their husbands to sell engines for mere money."

Which has happened. But after that, a steam engine man is finished. His eyes go dull. Therefore I would never get rid of my steam roller. In fact I have my eyes on a tractor which goes 16 miles an hour on rubber covered wheels. To me that represents a whole new dimension.

However getting back to steam engine men. I would meet them at fairs and rallies, then naturally ask them to my place for a drink and a chat like. Also, on the way to my place or to theirs, we would have a few drinks to while the travelling hours away.

I remember one instance when two of us were drinking and driving at 4 mph through the long night. The steam engine chap I had with me became so drunk he fell down at the back of the engine. He were a huge fellow, over six feet tall and wore size 15 boots which stuck out the end of the tarpaulin I put over him.

I was still trundling along quite happily when all of a sudden the quiet road became a hive of activity. Police cars kept appearing and skidding to a stop until they surrounded me. It were lucky I could stop as well and none of them got squashed. Then about a dozen policemen came towards me, all serious like, with the sergeant in charge the most serious of all. I thought,

'Fred, this is definitely it.'

So I though some more and before that very serious looking sergeant could have his say about my condition, the bottles rolling around the floor, not to speak of the unconscious figure, I asked him about my steam roller,

"Do you like these things?"

I must have been inspired. You should have seen his eyes light up. He was like a little lad all over again, a boy with a new toy. I went on, "Would you like a go?" and his eyes went even bigger. At last he spoke,

"Can I.. can I drive it?"

"You can't drive it," I said sternly, "but you may steer it. Under my supervision of course."

"Of course, of course," he said humbly, then helped me to shift the steam engine chap, who had begun snoring, out of our way. By that time all the other policemen were smiling and relaxed. I suppose it makes a change from heavy crime to come across a minor Victorian felon like me.

Well that sergeant and I went about four miles, which took an hour. We trundled up a long hill into town with the rest of the squad escorting us. By then it were dawn and the sun was rising. It shone on that sergeant's face and I have never seen anyone so happy. At last he turned to where I was sitting on the other side of my snoring friend and he said,

"Thank you. Thank you very much."

So I say to myself, steam engines cannot be that bad if they give people such pleasure. There have got to be worse things in life.

A steam engine also gives a kind of immortality, especially if you have resurrected one from a pile of rust. It does me good to know that after I am dead and gone, my steam roller will still be around. Even if some lunatic drops the bomb, it needs to be a powerful one to knock over Fred Dibnah's steam roller, I can tell you. Maybe the survivors will say,

"Let us connect up to that wheel there to do a bit of belting,' and they would be in buisness. They might build an engine house round my steam roller with a brick chimney above. As I have said, it is a strange world.

But getting back to the present, every year I go to the great steam engine rally at Chelford which is in the foreign fields of Cheshire. It is an epic journey with five hundred weight of coal under the beds, 80 gallons of water in the tank and a relentless pace of 4 miles an hour.

Usually I get this great pile up of cars behind me, though most seem to like steam rollers. Ever so often however there will be an impatient fellow hooting away somewhere along the line. That makes him a marked man as far as I am concerned. I know he is going to try overtaking the lot of us at the next straight stretch. I also know he will toot his little horn when accelerating past me.

I therefore watch his approach and, just when his car is going past, I blew my steam whistle at 200 pounds per square inch. It can be quite a shock to the nervous system.

To me, driving through the countryside is rather boring because of those fields. I was born and bred among streets, factories and chimneys, all of which are interesting and different, while one field looks like another. It is the same with trees. I can tell the difference between say, oak and elm, but one elm tree looks very much like another elm tree, especially when you are rolling past at walking pace.

Then there is the noise aspect. Some engines with worn gearing make it impossible to speak to anyone more than a foot away, except in sign language. Others are really noisy and you can hear them coming for miles. Imagine if you are driving such a machine. You are in a noisy world of your own.

Mine is not particularly bad but, after a few miles, it does leave me stone deaf. At least it has not done me any harm compared with the oil problems. The drops of oil being slung around get in your eyes making them sore. On the other hand it is a good way to know the engine is running properly. If the oil being spattered about turns from nice and warm to red hot, there could be trouble.

Too much sunshine is another source of trouble where steam engines are concerned. After a long run on a sunny day, everything becomes too hot to touch. Even the footplate turns into a sort of frying pan cooking your feet inside of their boots. That is why steam engine drivers prefer to travel in the pouring rain. They are under a good sized roof and the rain on the rest of the engine acts as a sort of water cooling system.

Unfortunately rain can cause another problem for steam rollers. Because there are no rubber tyres, the wheels and rollers will slip on wet hilly roads or when trying to stop. Going down hill can be bad especially if there are metal manhole covers. Once a steam roller starts skidding it becomes a monster. That is why I have good brakes on mine to keep it under control.

I have only had two near disasters with my steam roller. The first was when I had a surplus of stones which a very posh restaurant decided it wanted to buy—provided I could deliver. So I said to them,

"I'll deliver by steam power."

"You're joking." they said.

"I am not joking," I said, just to show them, I loaded a big trailer with all the stones.

Well the load came to 20 tons and I set off for this restaurant place which is some miles outside Bolton on the moors. The road is very steep— 1 in 7—which is like Everest for a steam roller. However I made the outer journey all right apart from burning the paint of the funnel.

It took some time to unload 20 tons and by then night was falling. So I lit the lamps and set out on the return journey. I thought getting back without the load would be simple. But, as I came travelling down that hill the crankshaft seemed to be going round a bit too fast. The next thing I knew was, instead of the wheels rolling properly, they were sliding like a sledge. I was tobogganing on a runaway steam roller from one side of the road to the other.

By then the speed had increased to 25 mph which for a steam roller is fearful. I knew that halfway down the hill there were a corner and I also knew there was no way I could get round it. When I reached the corner, my runaway monster went straight across the road and into a field. A flat field might have helped but this particular field had even more of a slant than the road.

At the far end of the field there was a 14 ft drop into the back of a geriatric hospital. Fortunately, I hit a stone pillar which shattered sending bits of rock high into the sky. My steam roller also shattered. The front of the boiler dug 18 inches in the ground. If the roller had got away it would have gone into the hospital like them bouncing bombs in the Dambusters.

My second near disaster, though it were not my fault, happened at the Chelford steam rally. Among other attractions they have stuntmen always looking for more sensational tricks.One came up to me and said he was an escapologist.

"I let people," he went on, "wrap 30 ft of chain round me and padlock the ends. Then I let them put me in a leather sack and padlock that. The trick I have in mind is—when I'm in the sack and lying in the middle of the arena—I want you to try and run over me with your steam roller."

"You must be mad." I said.

'No I'm not," he replied. "I can get out of the chains in seconds and escape from the leather sack anytime I want to. How long would it take your steam roller to reach the centre of the arena?"

"Twelve seconds at the most."

'No problem." he said.

Well I thought about it and I was a bit apprehensive like but the stunt man kept on at me. In the end we drew up a legal document saying that, if I squashed him flat, his widow would not sue me. He signed it at once and, after a couple more pints, so did I. But, as I sat on the steam roller watching the stunt man being chained, padlocked and put in the sack, I began to wonder what I had done. And would do.

They tell me the announcer made a big thing of the event and the crowd became very quiet, though I did not know due to the engine noise. Later Alison said she shut her eyes. I could not see much either because after six seconds the front of the vehicle blotted out my view of the wriggling man in the sack. He escaped by rolling to one side at the last second—still in the sack.

I suppose stunt men get their kicks, not so much because of the money, but from the danger then the applause. I suppose I am a bit like that with my chimneys and steam engines. That afternoon at the Chelford rally, Fred Dibnah won a special prize for possessing the steam vehicle that had travelled the greatest distance under its own power.

In the end I think of the friends I have made through steam engines. I generally meet them when grovelling in the road filling up with water. After that I have to call on them year after year and we become friends for life. They insist on giving me cans of beer, which I cannot refuse, also they seem to like me going into their posh houses to use their toilets.

Chapter 9

The Rest of Fred

I am a Victorian. I don't do things like going shopping, you know. I went into a shop the other day and I had to walk out. I got that upset with the woman behind the counter.

Traction engines are good things because they don't answer you back. You can belt them with a hammer and they say nowt.

Fred and Alison stop for a drink on a Sunday afternoon outing, with 'Alison'.

Having steam engines for a hobby makes a lot of work. Often I am in my workshop until one in the morning. After nine at night, I contain my hammering. At least I leave off the heavy blows out of respect for my neighbours.

Donald who lives 200 yards aways says he can hear them in his parlour. So I have to think about my nearest neighbour who is only 20 yards away. Mind you his house is up for sale.

There was a steeplejack called Mr. Smith and he lived in Rochdale from about 1860-1905. In those days the chimney around Lancashire were like blades of grass, which made it the golden age of steeplejacking.

This fellow Smith christened himself the Lancashire Steeplejack. He claimed to be the man who invented the method of scaling a factory chimney. It is quite possibly true. Before 1850, chimneys were about 90 feet high, then the Victorians began to build 2-300 footers. By the end of the century they needed mending and steeplejacks had a lot of trouble climbing them.

At Bolton we had the biggest chimney in England. It was 34 feet wide at the top, 127 feet in circumference at the base and 369 feet tall. There was only one other taller chimney in the whole of the British Isles—the Townsend chimney at Glasgow. That was 490 feet tall. I would have liked to climb it.

During the 1970's there were government sponsored people calling themselves church cleaners. They would arrive, encase the church in scaffolding, break a million slates and shoot steam all over the place. They did more damage in 10 years than a 100 years of industrial activity.

In the town of Haywood they had England's answer to the leaning tower of Pisa. It were a 200 ft factory chimney that was 5 ft out of plumb. At one time this was the wonder of Lancashire. It stood there for years and its owners were rather proud of the freak thing. I don't know who knocked it down but it's gone now.

One fellow used to specialise in straightening curved chimneys. This was by no means an easy feat because, if anything went wrong, you could not run out of the way.

He did this by cutting a series of horizontal slots then, with the help of iron wedges, putting thicker bricks on the convex side and narrower bricks on the other. He were a sort of inspired lunatic.

Thunder and lightning can scare you a bit. On one occasion I was up a 200 ft chimney from which there was a rope down to the ground. Rain had been falling all night and the rope was sopping wet.

Suddenly I heard this kind of bang and the electricty travelled down that rope to the ground like along a high tension cable. It were enough for me. I went down the ladders almost as fast.

On another occasion I was up a church spire in a storm. Eventually I shot off the spire and inside the tower, but that was still 100 ft high. There was banging and crashing outside as if someone was trying to get at me crouching up there in the belfry. When the storm has passed over I went outside again and touched the lightning conductor. I nearly jumped back off the spire for the conductor was nearly red hot.

It was half past eight on a Sunday morning at a place called Prescot near Liverpool. We had spent the Saturday preparing to demolish a dodgy 150 ft chimney and I were surprised it had not fallen over during the night. As Donald and I were on our final preparations a policeman came up and asked,

"Have you ever had any that went wrong?" People love disasters you know.

"Well," said Donald, "on average one in every four go wrong, and we've just done three good ones.

Now that I have finished 14 years hard work on this steam roller I keep having funny thoughts about buying another one. It must have springs and rubber tyres though because metal rollers conk your teeth out going over manhole covers.

A steam tractor, compared with the roller, will have a little axle up front with two wheels on it. Then there would be big wheels at the back. They would make it romp along with half the pain.

Now I think I can afford to buy a wreck and do it up like I did the last one. Those that are already done up and painted cost £15,000 which I can't afford.

Traction engines travel at about 16 miles an hour, which is four times faster than my steam roller. So I shall be able to get to rallies before my old age and not pop off on the way.

You have got to be a bit crackers to work on steam engines. It kills a lot of men off. Quite a few start with a great deal of enthusiasm. They are going to do this and that during the winter in preparation for next year's steam fairs. Which means working nights in sheds like I do. After the first nasty winter, it is sort of bonk, and they have gone.

I am a compulsive cigarette smoker, you know. I have to celebrate with a cigarette and when everything goes right on a job, I am smoking all the time.

Terrible things happen to cigarette smokers up chimneys. Like you have a packet of 20 in your top pocket, bend a bit and you see it floating down straight into a puddle of water. That sort of stops me going down 200 ft for another packet.

Matches are another problem. When I am out of them I send a special signal to Donald who sticks three in the rope. Trouble is they tend to strike themselves on the side of the chimney on the way up.

Then, having managed to light a cigerette, it is gone in a couple of minutes. You can see it glowing at the end because of the wind. Smoking is therefore a bit of a hazard but so is climbing chimneys.

All the old steeplejacks used to smoke. They would sit halfway up and have a puff, so I do the same. It is a wonderful sensation to put your back against the wall, halfway up to heaven as you might say. I think about what I am going to do with my steam engine at home and about the big problem awaiting me at the top of the chimney. I have solved a lot of them having a cigarette halfway up.

There are some unexpected hazards working up church towers and steeples. More often than not a nesting bird will come zooming out of somewhere. I treat them with the greatest respect because I know one of the damn things could kill me. It could happen in a split second. Next thing I could be rattling down the side of the church breaking of a few fancy bits on my way. After that I would have half a day out with the undertakers.

I believe in God. Sometimes I have a feeling he might know me like. 'That's Fred Dibnah,' he would say, 'who keeps climbing my church spires.' Some days he does not like me. I drive 20 miles, climb 200 feet and his heavens open.

On the other hand, he has not let me fall off so far or let me drop anything to kill anybody. My wife Alison says, 'You'll never fall off. There's definitely somebody watching you somewhere.' She says I am better up aloft than on the floor. Quite often I trip over things on floors.

My sort of heaven would be a great place where nobody did any fighting or was hungry. In my part I would like a big pile of rusty steam engines and enough iron plate to mend them.

That would be quite wonderful because I would not have to worry where my next dinner was coming from. I could just get on mending those ancient relics forever.

Some church vicars get in a bit of a huff with me.

'You have had the job for weeks,'' they say. 'When are you going to get on with it?''

Unfortunately my job does not work their way. You see, they are speaking from the comfort and warmth of a vestry. They do not seem to realise it rains, blows and snows outside. So quite a lot send me letters starting,

"Dear Mr Dibnah, if you feel you cannot get around to doing my job, I shall have to find someone else."

I do not say much as their church spires have been falling to pieces or collecting pidgeon shit for the last 20 years.

I rather like my oily flat cap. People ask me what is its flash point which isn't a joke really. When I am working with hot iron, it does go on fire at times and I have to whack out the flames.

If I go on holiday I find I must wear my cap or I feel as if somebody has shaved my head. Also, after days slogging over steam engines, I have actually been to bed in it. I also wear it going to the toilet. Well, Mark Phillips wears a cap doesn't he?

On one occasion I put rather a big dent on top of a brand new motor car. It should not have been parked in my brick disposal area round the bottom of a chimney. So it was not my fault. I had picked up two bricks then the wind took off a nice ¾ inch thick bed of mortar. The piece went sailing away on the wind in a most beautiful arc before landing up on this fellow's new Volvo. He was not too happy.

I am sort of insured but if I kill any insurance officials looking up at me from down below, I am in dire trouble. It would be fair to say insurance men and me don't mix. To them I am a bit like those racing drivers or that chap who jumps off cliffs on his motor bike. High risk they call it which means jacking premiums up. Still it makes them rich.

I'll never be a rich man climbing chimneys. There is no doubt about that. I would be better off owning a corner shop. On the other hand I am never broke because there is always somebody wanting me to do something silly. Like risking my neck.

I don't count money. I spend it as it comes. Alison can have what she wants and my steam engine called Alison is real greedy. Always wanting money. Fortunately I think steam engines are better than money, like some people prefer old stamps or oil paintings.

This celebrity business is all very well if you could escape from it. For example I never thought it took so many man-hours to make an advertisement for beer. We did 999 takes of me drinking beer in some club. I had to take a taxi home afterwards as my legs wouldn't work.

Often I get fantastic phone calls such as would I hop over to Barbados and knock 50 feet off a couple of chimneys. Donald said he disliked camping so we did not go. Anyway me knees are knobbly and I would not look very good in shorts.

I built a chimney for me mum when I was 17 years old. We had a stack like the one next door. Four out of five pots were disused so I concentrated on making one good stack. I did not really design it, just built it. People said I was crazy but it never cracked and has a strong draught that would suck your slippers off.

My main competition when it comes to felling chimneys is from the dynamite men. They come along, press a plunger, bang and that's it. Or there are the mad men. No pit props, nothing. They chop a hole out of the bottom, like the chimney were a tree. They keep bashing away when it is creaking and groaning, then they run out the road at great speed.

What they have done is they have just destroyed something which took a lot of men a long time, hard work, blood and sweat to construct. When those old builders finished the job, they were proud to place a Union Jack on the top. If you had, like I do, to take out three foot of brick when a few hundred tons is squeezing on it, then that chimney has not died so easy, has it?

I said I did not go much on insurance men. They send some lad out from the office, who has never seen a chimney before, to work out all the risks involved. I ask you. Yet they have got big new Mk 10 Jaguars which they park next to my second hand army Land Rover. There is a moral in that somewhere.

Some funny jobs come my way because I have this reputation for working quietly and systematically. The local authority called me one day and asked if I would help them with a nature reserve.

"We want you," they said, "to lower an island without shattering the tranquillity of the place."

You see, the nature reserve was being created in an old valley where there was wild fowl that have short legs and webbed feet. The fowl could not get on to the island on account of its sides being too steep.

"Oh I see," I said when this was explained to me. "You want it levelling out a bit—like Blackpool—so they can just wander off the beach."

"That's right," said the nature chap.

At one time the valley had been thick with coal mines, then it became a tip full of rubbish, rats and flies. When the wind was blowing, you needed a gas mask to go near the place. Now all is covered over by beautiful green grass and trees have been planted. In 20 years time it will be as if men had never mucked it up in the first place.

So there I was helping things along. I had to reduce the height of the island from its present 15 ft tall to 3 foot. It would have been easier to blow off the top by explosives but the fishes and wild fowl would not have liked that. Therefore I did it silently, the old fashioned way, with a shovel.

Sometimes when I am high up some chimney or church tower, I get illusions of grandeur. I look down on those humble rows of houses and say,

"I am glad I'm up here and not down there inside one of your little places. Up here I am as free as a bird."

I often think my sort of life is more exciting than most people's. They never have anything exciting unless they go on strike.

Perhaps steeplejacking appeals to me because I am basically lazy. It is the sort of job where some days, when it rains, I am quite happy. You see it means I can stay home and work on my engines. Time passes pleasantly by that way.

Now if I were working a machine in a factory I would watch the clock all the time. People often ask if I am not bored knocking them bricks off one at a time. Well, the answer is no.

Because parts of my job are relatively simple, I carry on doing them while my mind wanders away to pleasant things—like I am at home mending steam engines.

I think I'll die when nobody wants me no more. But I also think I'll carry on until I am an old fellow. I don't know but I suppose I'll slow down before I am 70. Instead of dying in bed I would like to drop off something on a nice sunny day and that would be that.

Near my house is the cemetery where we all end up eventually. In there somewhere is the first and only man in Bolton to be killed by a lion, which is interesting. Also me dad used to tell me interesting stories about the place. How, when there was a great flood, one or two bodies were washed into the river. I don't know if there is any truth in it but I do know that in the river bed there are all sorts of gravestones.

I would not mind building my own grave stone. It would be like a chimney with a staging round the top, lightning conductor and everything. Carved on it could be just—Fred.

The smoking debris of the former chimney at Era Mill, Rochdale.